Instant
NEGOTIATION

BRIAN CLEGG

KOGAN
PAGE

To all the salesmen who have taught me the hard way

First published in 2000

Apart from any fair dealing for the purposes of research or private study, or criticism or review, as permitted under the Copyright, Designs and Patents Act 1988, this publication may only be reproduced, stored or transmitted, in any form or by any means, with the prior permission in writing of the publishers, or in the case of reprographic reproduction in accordance with the terms and licences issued by the CLA. Enquiries concerning reproduction outside these terms should be sent to the publishers at the undermentioned addresses:

Kogan Page Limited
120 Pentonville Road
London
N1 9JN
UK

Stylus Publishing Inc.
22883 Quicksilver Drive
Sterling
VA 20166-2012
USA

© Brian Clegg, 2000

The right of Brian Clegg to be identified as the author of this work has been asserted by him in accordance with the Copyright, Designs and Patents Act 1988.

British Library Cataloguing in Publication Data

A CIP record for this book is available from the British Library.

ISBN 0 7494 3387 6

Typeset by Jo Brereton, Primary Focus, Haslington, Cheshire
Printed and bound in Great Britain by Clays Ltd, St Ives plc

Contents

1 Negotiation 1

The human condition	3
What's it all for?	3
The mythical win–win	4
Are they the opposition?	5
Strategy versus tactics	5
Intuition versus logic	6
Process versus communications	7

2 Strategy versus tactics 9

What sort of relationship?	11
The one-off	11
The long term	12
Knowing it all	13
Knowing your opponent	14
Knowing your deal	15
Setting targets	15
Are they telling the truth?	16
Sensitive to the moment	17
Widening the picture	18
Getting time right	19

3 Intuition versus logic 21

A balance	23
Using emotion	23
Dealing with people	24
Culture shock	25
Type profiles and horoscopes	26
Dealing with stress	27
Building trust	28
A little endorsement	29
Evaluating options	29
Going with the gut	30

4 Process versus communications   33

The balance	35
The matter of price	35
There's always another lever	36
Your USP	36
Listening	37
Talking	37
Assertive or aggressive?	38
Establishing a direction	39
Plotting out the journey	40

5 The exercises   41

5.1	Lifetime value	43
5.2	Taking notes	44
5.3	Web research	45
5.4	The agreement space	46
5.5	Hearing what they really say	48
5.6	Are they telling the truth?	49
5.7	Upping the game	50
5.8	Paper mountains	51
5.9	Talking yourself down	52
5.10	Waiting room	53
5.11	Go casual	54
5.12	Using emotion	55
5.13	Competitive pressure	56
5.14	Breathing is good for you	57
5.15	The power of print	58
5.16	It's yours right now	59
5.17	Getting endorsements	60
5.18	Exploring trust	61
5.19	Basic option evaluation	62
5.20	Sophisticated option evaluation	63
5.21	Options with guts	64
5.22	Reading upside down (no, really!)	65
5.23	Starting prices	66
5.24	Playing poker	67
5.25	Another lever	68
5.26	Your USP	69
5.27	Setting targets	70
5.28	Play that back	71
5.29	Subverting a meeting	72
5.30	Knowing the opposition	73
5.31	Broken CD	74
5.32	Cut the aggro	75

5.33	Which way?	76
5.34	Terms of endearment	77
5.35	Future visions	78
5.36	I'll be honest…	79
5.37	When you lose your temper	80
5.38	Creative negotiation	81
5.39	Beautiful barter	82
5.40	Delightful deals	83
5.41	Personality types	84
5.42	Wooing them	85
5.43	Selling your wider strengths	86
5.44	Common ground	87
5.45	Rehearsing for success	88
5.46	Yes… eventually	89
5.47	Little successes	90
5.48	Slowing the pace	91
5.49	Throwing in the condiment	92
5.50	Deadlines – the movable feast	93
5.51	Remote negotiation	95
5.52	Make them feel good about the deal	96
5.53	Plotting the journey	97
5.54	Using silence	98
5.55	Cornered rats	99
5.56	Ask, ask and ask again	100
5.57	Coffee and doughnuts	101
5.58	Body language	102
5.59	Don't leave the next step in their hands	103
5.60	Say what?	104
5.61	You won't win them all	105
5.62	Principles	106
5.63	Aim high to get more	107
5.64	There's always an 'if'	108
5.65	Knowing your products and services	109
5.66	Doing a special	110
5.67	Slicing the salami	111
5.68	Walkies!	112
5.69	Good guy/bad guy	113
5.70	I haven't the authority…	114
5.71	Appearing naïve	115
5.72	Liking the opposition	116
5.73	Stakeholder customer	117
5.74	Being you	118
5.75	Price movement	119

6 Other sources 121

    Finding out more   123

Appendix: The selector 129

    Selection tables   131
    The random selector   131
    Techniques in timing order   132
    Techniques in frequency order   133
    Techniques by strategic rating   134
    Techniques by intuitive rating   135
    Techniques by process rating   136
    Techniques by fun rating   137

1

NEGOTIATION

THE HUMAN CONDITION

It's hard to imagine business – or even life – without negotiation. Practically every business interaction, from the largest corporate merger to a meeting to decide the site of a new bicycle shed, depends on negotiation. In fact, it's rare to find any human transaction at all where there isn't some room for discussion and modification of terms.

The good negotiator has to call on a whole raft of skills. He or she needs to be an effective communicator, combining the abilities to sell and to listen. The negotiator must be able to balance tactical and strategic considerations. Good negotiators know their business and their company inside out – and know just as much about the other side, too. As if this isn't enough, good negotiators also need flexibility – the ability to explore what is possible, changing goal from a hypothetical summit to a more reachable hill.

There is good news and bad news here. Many of the skills of negotiation cannot be learned without practice. But this doesn't mean that you have to plunge a virgin negotiator into a corporate merger. Every day you are negotiating – at home, on the way to work, in the office. Negotiation is a natural part of life. With the Instant approach of gradually building a toolkit of techniques it is possible to use everyday life as your negotiating workshop, integrating new skills piece by piece.

Like the other books in the series, *Instant Negotiation* has a few short introductory chapters, then the main section comprising of more than 70 exercises, each taking five to 20 minutes, which can be used to improve negotiating skills. Each exercise has a star rating showing positioning on the three scales – strategic, intuitive and process (plus a fun rating).

WHAT'S IT ALL FOR?

Before plunging into the 'how' of negotiation, it's worth taking a brief step back and look at the 'why'. What is the point of the exercise? Why negotiate at all? From either side of a negotiation, there is a practical need. If you are selling (in the widest sense of the word), you want to get the best price with the best terms. If you are buying you also want the best price and terms, but strangely this now means something quite different. Some negotiations are more about finding an agreed version of reality rather than buying and selling, but even here points of view will drive parties to pull the result in a particular direction.

Negotiations can be distinguished from other forms of social interaction by the fact that there is a specific, pre-identified, desired outcome. It might be a purchase or a pay deal, it might be where to go for dinner or how late a child can stay out at night. The desired outcome is to reach agreement on the subject, but each party in the negotiation has their own slant on what would be the best flavour of outcome. Each is trying to move the result into their own preferred solution space.

It should never be forgotten, however, when dealing with negotiations that this remains a social interaction between human beings. Mechanical 'negotiations' can be disastrous. The unbending application of a series of rules can make a negotiation run out of control, never getting to a conclusion. Negotiation is not a pure science – it is a blend of logic and emotion, of gut feel and calculation. Neither the human nor the calculated side is enough on its own. There is a need for both.

THE MYTHICAL WIN–WIN

There's a magic goal that features in every book written on negotiation: the mystic state of win–win. The concept is very simple: that both parties (or all the parties if there are more than two) go away from a negotiation feeling positive about the outcome. Win–win is usually highly desirable, for reasons we will explore in a few moments, but first let's deal with the alternatives.

It's not necessary to spend long over one option: lose–win. The position where the opposition wipes the floor with you is not one that many companies or individuals would seriously contemplate as a negotiating strategy – unless the aim is self-destruction. However, there is a certain attraction to win–lose. When I was first involved in negotiation, dealing with suppliers for a corporate's PC and software purchasing, I sat alongside a purchasing professional whose sole aim in life seemed to be to achieve win–lose. Being relatively young and innocent at the time, I have to admit that I found this a natural approach, and even got quite a thrill out of squeezing our suppliers until the pips squeaked.

Unfortunately there are real dangers in win–lose. If a large company is negotiating with a much smaller one, the big player is in a position of power because of relative size. In their eagerness to get the contract, the small company might accept a win–lose outcome that is disastrous to them financially. It doesn't do anyone any good to put their suppliers or customers out of business. Taking win–lose to this extreme is simply disruptive.

Similarly, if you intend to have any long-term relationship with the other company or individual, it is dangerous to push them until their backs are against the wall. They will resent it, and the result will be a working relationship without trust that is a constant struggle. The only time you might consider going for broke is in a one-off negotiation. For example, when buying a house, it is very unlikely you will ever buy off that same person again. Here's a circumstance where win–lose may be worth pursuing.

On the whole, though, it is win–win that is most desirable. Here, all the parties to the negotiation feel that they have got something positive. No one is disappointed. There is an opportunity to build a workable relationship. The win–win outcome is often achievable if you aim for it, but not so often by accident. Planning for win–win is an important part of achieving success.

Bear in mind, of course, that there are many degrees of win–win. It doesn't mean splitting the difference. It doesn't mean that both sides gain identical, balanced advantages. You are still in this for what you can get, but aiming to do it in an ethical way that leaves the other side satisfied. Maybe just not so satisfied as you.

ARE THEY THE OPPOSITION?

When writing about negotiation there is an immediate problem. How do we refer to the other people involved in the negotiation? It's easy to refer to them as the opposition. After all, unless there are some areas of conflict and disagreement, there really isn't any negotiation, just a celebration of completion. Yet there's a real danger of getting into a mindset that makes win–win impossible. You don't go for win–win with the opposition, you go out to demolish them.

Unfortunately, there is no easy term for the other parties. It's tempting to call them and think of them as partners – but this makes the relationship too chummy. Yes, you hope that you can achieve an outcome that will be satisfactory for everyone, but in the end it's your own goals that matter most. Perhaps all partnerships are really like this, but the word has enough inappropriate connotations to make it unsuitable.

Debating the word to use isn't just a matter of semantics. Once you think of the people on the other side of the table as 'the opposition', you can't help but adopt a mind-set that pushes away from win–win. I have to admit to not having an ideal solution to this problem. I have resorted to the word 'stakeholder' as being someone who has an interest (a stake) in the negotiation. It is a more neutral word than opposition or partner and will have to do.

STRATEGY VERSUS TACTICS

Strategy and tactics are terms that tend to be used extremely loosely these days. Both are applied casually to any planning for future action. But in negotiation, each has a clear meaning. Your strategy defines the position you are aiming to achieve, your planned target and goals. Strategy is not about a specific negotiating session, but about the direction of the whole enterprise. Tactics, on the other hand, remain very firmly rooted in the human interaction of negotiation itself. Your tactics will be the actual words and figures you use, your stance, your manner, your ploys and gambits.

Rather confusingly, the same two terms can also be applied to the scope of your relationship with the other stakeholders in this negotiation. If this is a one-off negotiation, where win–lose is a possible sensible approach, you could call this a tactical negotiation. There is no long-term consideration. It doesn't matter how the other people feel about you, as long as you get the right outcome. On the other hand, if this negotiation is part of a long-term relationship, then the scope of the negotiation has to go beyond the mere tactics of 'How do I get the absolute best deal today?' to the strategy of 'How do I make the most out of this long-term relationship?' This strategic viewpoint is very different from the tactical.

Both these interpretations are used in this book when looking at the strategic/ tactical dimension, as it is often impractical in reality to separate the two.

INTUITION VERSUS LOGIC

Human relationships sit at the heart of negotiation. Inherent in this fact is the balance of intuition and logic. However you look at the human approach to life you can see two strong factors, each beneficial, each limited. In creative terms they are often referred to as left brain and right brain, after the now largely discredited theory that each way of thinking and acting is largely dependent on the relevant lobe of the brain. The labels, though, remain useful.

Left-brain thinking is logical, calculating and structured. It deals with numbers and words. It is analytical, unemotional and lacking in creativity. Right-brain thinking is more intuitive and extravagant. It deals with images and concepts, links and ideas. It is flavoured by emotion and coloured by mood. It is much more holistic and original.

When being creative in business we need both types of activity. Left brain to assess the requirement and understand the background. Right brain to come up with great new ideas and solve problems. Left brain to select from those ideas and make them practical. Right brain to combine and improve on the ideas. Left brain to put them into practice. Although this is presented as an alternation, in practice we usually need a mix of both modes, with one dominant at any one time.

Exactly the same dynamic tension exists in negotiation. You need a good grasp of the facts and figures, a good picture of the positions on both sides of the negotiation – logical, fact based, left brain. You need to be flexible and sensitive to mood, to come up with new ways of approaching the outcome that might prove win–win – intuitive, gut-feel based, right brain, and so on. This mix of the intuitive and the logical is what makes human beings so irritating to deal with – and so enjoyable.

Don't think, however, that this is an unfortunate mix and that everything would be just fine if only it were possible to eliminate the intuitive side and manage only on logic. It is the balance of intuition and logic, of right and left brain, that is needed for good negotiation. With intuition alone the process will be unstructured and will become an argument or a fight. With logic alone there will be no way out of the inevitable impasse. The negotiation will either spiral to nothing or simply not get anywhere. Both are essential.

PROCESS VERSUS COMMUNICATIONS

The final dimension depends on the fundamental activities of negotiating. Much of it is concerned with process. The mechanics of deciding which variables to manipulate, the calculation of which option to push for, the setting of direction and route. But these are primarily solitary activities, and as I never tire of mentioning, negotiation is at its core a human interaction. So alongside the process considerations sits the need for effective communication – to listen and speak effectively, to persuade and to influence.

Because communication is a touchy-feely subject where process sounds mechanistic, it is tempting to align these two with our other dimension of logic versus intuition. To do so is a mistake. Some aspects of communication can be planned and logical with every word crafted with a particular intent in mind. Similarly, a process like evaluating options can only go so far on logic – in the end it is gut feel that drives most business decisions, so there is nothing strange about a logical communication or an intuitive process.

The importance of the process versus communication dimension will be explored further in Chapter 4, but for the next chapter we will focus on strategy and tactics.

2

STRATEGY VERSUS TACTICS

WHAT SORT OF RELATIONSHIP?

As we have already seen, strategy and tactics come into negotiation in two ways. They involve the nature of your association with the other stakeholders in the relationship – is it a one-off interaction, or will it be a long-term relationship? They also cover the difference between your goals in undertaking the negotiation and the specific methods used on the day to negotiate. In both cases, the dividing factor is time. Strategy takes the long-term view, tactics the on-the-day, now or never aspect.

In this chapter we will be examining both aspects of the division between strategy and tactics in more detail.

THE ONE-OFF

Let's begin with the frequency issue, specifically the one-off negotiation. Here strategy and tactics fuse into one. The long-term view is the short-term view, because there is no long term. Your goal has to be what you get out of the session – because there won't be another chance. Of course not all one-off negotiations involve a single negotiating session. You can have a single goal with multiple meetings (for instance, selling a house), but with less significant deals a single session might be your only chance for success.

This one-off nature gives a special freedom to be a little more dramatic than usual. You may feel that it is appropriate to go for broke – to push for a win–lose. The easiest examples are those involving simple sales, but the lessons apply whatever the negotiation. For instance, buying a house you could offer not 10 per cent under the asking price, but half the asking price. Sometimes it will be accepted. Often it won't, but at least you can guarantee plenty of leeway in your negotiating position.

Similarly, if someone had a valuable antique for sale that you recognized and they didn't, you might offer a paltry sum in the hope that it would be sold to you as the junk its owner obviously thought it was. Or in a business contract negotiation you might force through a wide range of conditions, holding some bargaining counter over the other stakeholders' heads. In the 1980s and 1990s, it was not unusual for negotiations with organized labour to be pushed into a win–lose position by a combination of legislation and heavy handedness. Unfortunately, of course, these weren't generally one-off negotiations, so they were often storing up trouble for the company concerned.

The aversion to win–lose isn't a matter of weakness and not trying to get the best deal for your side, just an acceptance that, where possible, it makes sense to ensure that everyone gets something and goes away happy. That makes for smoother business – and why shouldn't you make people happy if you can? There is a moral dilemma involved in some of these negotiations. While people often enjoy boasting how they bought something valuable for a pittance, there is a considerable moral imperative to give the vendor a more reasonable amount – not necessarily full market value, but an amount that isn't laughable – out of common humanity. Negotiation is a matter for human beings, not robots.

Remember, also, that one-off deals cut both ways. If you are too hard in your bargaining it is quite possible that the other parties will pull out – and then you may regret your daring. It is also quite likely that the one-off nature was an illusion, accidentally or intentionally. It could be that because of changes of circumstances you need to deal with the same person again. I know of, for instance, someone who was really unpleasant to the boss who had made him redundant. He made his negotiations on redundancy as difficult as possible for the boss. A while later he got a job for another firm, only to find out that in the meanwhile his previous boss had also moved to that firm. He had the doubtful pleasure of being made redundant twice in two years by the same man. How much the second event was influenced by previous negotiations is hard to say, but it would be very naïve to suggest there was no possible connection.

It may also be the case that, despite all the signs, you are being tried out for a longer relationship. A company might negotiate a one-off deal with no suggestion that there is anything more to it. If they are treated well, they may later (knowingly) come back to establish a long-term contract. Go into that one-off deal with the intention of taking them for everything they've got and that long-term contract could well be in jeopardy.

So feel free to be hard on someone whose house you are buying, or whose assets you are buying up when his company leaves the country – but make sure you have done your homework and minimized the chances of this backfiring. Imagine, for instance, using rather dubious tactics to sell a house at maximum profit, only to find next week that the person you sold it to was a major customer of your business. And she wanted a meeting with you about business ethics. Time to hide under the desk.

THE LONG TERM

Handling a negotiation that is part of a long-term relationship is a very different affair. Here lifetime value becomes a crucial component of the consideration. The other stakeholders may continue to influence your life and business for a long time to come. In reaching a negotiation you have to consider not only what you can get today, but how that outcome will influence future negotiations and relationships.

If you have the total upper hand – let's say you are a political dictator with enormous powers – you may feel that this is irrelevant because you are always going to be in charge. History has some important lessons that you shouldn't ignore, though. Most dictators find that their power cannot be sustained forever, and then the results of earlier negotiations may come home to roost. You may not actually be running a country, but even someone in a position of power in a company or simply with 'yes' or 'no' authority in a negotiation should consider that this degree of control may not stay with them for life – at some point, the boot may be on the other foot.

In most negotiations, though, we are not in a position of absolute power and the long-term view means that win–win becomes a golden opportunity. If you can reach an outcome that all parties consider to be positive, then each will go away from the negotiation in a better state for future relationships to flourish.

Because of the uncertainty of the future, the long-term view should be the default stance when looking at negotiating. Unless you can be reasonably sure that there will be no future comeback, your aim should be to establish win–win (though, of course, win–win that particularly benefits you).

KNOWING IT ALL

A major strategic weapon in handling negotiations is to be well prepared beforehand. The nature of negotiation is to have movement. If no movement occurs in a negotiation, in effect you haven't negotiated, you have just talked at each other. To be able to deal with such movement, to be able to continue to put your case given the changing circumstances, you will need to know not only your starting point, but the territory surrounding it.

The catalogue of information the good negotiator needs will obviously vary hugely from negotiation to negotiation, but the essence of the requirement is to minimize the risk of needing a piece of information on the spot and being unable to access it. Some fundamentals are to know just what is being negotiated, what your goals as a stakeholder in the negotiation are and what your variables are – the aspects of the negotiation that can be changed to produce an acceptable output.

However, these basics are just the starting point. Let's take three specific examples: as a buyer, a seller, and when negotiating to end an industrial dispute.

As a buyer you will need to know what you want to buy, how many, and what you want to do with the products or services (and when and where). You will want to know what a typical market price is, what you would like to pay, and what is the absolute maximum you would pay. You will want to know what alternatives there are to using this particular product or service – and what would happen if you didn't buy it at all. You will want to know about any existing or past contracts for related products and services, and about any needs you might have to get new contracts for related products and services. You will need to know the state of your company's (or personal) finances, plus the health of your cash flow and your credit worthiness.

As a seller you will need to know about all your products and services, not just the ones you are intending to sell today. You will need to know the published price, what you would like to get for the product, and what you can accept at rock bottom. You will need to know what your stock levels are, how you will deliver the products or services, and how you could handle particularly small or large orders. You will need to know your customer's credit worthiness and the state of their business. You will need to know everything there is to know about your potential customer's current relationship with your company – all the past deals, anything that has gone wrong (or particularly well). You had also better know plenty about your competitors' products and services. Know where you are better, but also know where they are, and be prepared to admit it (with a way to catch up and better them), rather than be surprised by, or simply deny, your competitors' good points.

When negotiating an end to an industrial dispute you will need to know the history of the dispute. You will need to know as much as possible about each party involved, both personally and in a work context. You will need to know both the alleged grievances and any possible underlying causes that are not formally on the table. You will need to know the directions in which each stakeholder can move. And you will need to know what each party has to be politically seen not to give away, even if in reality they do.

And those are just the generics. There will be other categories of information that will be specific to your company and business. The negotiator, or his or her support staff, needs to really know the company and the requirement inside out. Why do you need so much? You can't tell in which direction the discussions will move. If, for instance, you were trying to sell staples to a company and they said 'You already sell us pencils – can we do some kind of bundled deal', you would not be in a very good position if you didn't know about existing deals, and your company's other product lines (even if personally you only ever dealt in staples). Flexibility is an essential for good negotiation, and flexibility means knowing which way it's safe to move, and which way it isn't.

KNOWING YOUR OPPONENT

That's not the end of it. You might know your side of the negotiation perfectly, but you also need to know as much as you can about the other stakeholders. That is very obvious in the industrial dispute example above, but less so in the buying and selling examples. Here the seller needs to know as much as possible of the set of information the buyer needs to know. About other vendors they deal with, about other requirements they might have, and so on. Similarly, the good negotiator on the buying side needs to know the vendor inside out – and the vendor's competitors.

Arguably, this knowledge of the other stakeholders is more important than all but the most basic information about your own side. You will usually be able to pull together most internal information quickly if required. Information about the other parties may take longer to obtain.

This isn't really the place to go into how you obtain that information. The spectrum runs from published public information to illegally obtaining industrial secrets. I am not (the lawyers will be pleased to know) advocating the latter. However, it is quite feasible to go beyond what is published (say) in the other stakeholders' reports and accounts without doing anything legally risky.

An increasing amount of information is available about almost any subject on the Web (see the Research section of Chapter 6 on page 125). Companies specializing in information can give you vast amounts of detail on another company. You can talk to other third parties about their experiences. You can even approach the stakeholders directly – often they will be happy to give you information, although, of course, anything stated unofficially needs to be taken with a pinch of salt. The main thing is that the attempt is made. You might not get everything, but you will surprised just how much you can find out about the other stakeholders if you do try – and how valuable it can be.

A key requirement here is to keep your eyes open. Observing the other stakeholders, how they behave and any documentation you are shown will help. Sometimes you may see something accidentally. I recently went into a gift shop. While I was waiting to be served, I noticed a paper on the counter. As a habitual reader, my eyes flicked along the text as I waited. (It was upside down, but reading at a reasonable speed upside down is definitely a negotiating skill – see *Reading upside down*, 5.22). This document told me the mark-up on each of a number of products the shop sold. Such information, innocently obtained, might have been very valuable if I happened to be in negotiation with that shop.

KNOWING YOUR DEAL

Movement means you have to have a wide knowledge of your company and your products, and your competitors and the other stakeholders. But movement also has another impact on the knowledge required. You need to know the deal itself. Because if your picture is of the state of negotiations yesterday and things have moved on since then, you may end up arguing from the wrong position and giving way unnecessarily. I have seen a buyer reinstate a starting price after his colleagues had knocked it down to two thirds, simply by not being on top of the deal. It lost the company a hefty sum of money.

This is not usually a problem in a small, quick negotiation, where the position and any variables can easily be held in the heads of any stakeholders. But where the whole deal is complex, with many variables and perhaps many stakeholders, simply keeping a clear picture of the state of the deal is an essential for effective negotiation.

SETTING TARGETS

On the ground, dealing with the tactics of negotiation, there isn't time to assess every possibility and decide whether or not a particular suggestion from another stakeholder is acceptable. To make this tactical operation more practical, another strategic essential is to set targets. These should be clear, simple and quantifiable.

Targets need to specify what your ideal goals are in undertaking the negotiation. They should also define your room for manoeuvre. Where appropriate, it may be helpful to have this in the form of a table or chart, making it easy to combine a number of variables and to see how you are doing against target. For instance, if your variables on a sale included quantities, price, delivery cost, timing and bundled consumables, you might want to know what cut in price you would be happy with if the customer took twice as much product over a longer timescale. This shouldn't need to be a tactical consideration – good strategic target setting would mean that you could read off a ballpark response to a set of figures.

ARE THEY TELLING THE TRUTH?

Some aspects of negotiation are purely tactical though – never more so than the assessment of just what it is that the other stakeholders are telling you. It might be very foolish for them to tell you absolutely everything up front, but this is quite different from telling you lies. Once you suspect a stakeholder of lying, it is very difficult to continue the negotiation as if nothing had happened. Yet, initially, this is probably the best policy, as an apparent lie does not have to be what it seems.

Even if the stakeholder is telling an intentional untruth, there is a whole spectrum you need to be aware of. It could be an out-and-out lie to get business – 'We can deliver all of that three weeks ahead of the competition', but actually the company has neither the ability nor the will to do so. Car salesmen are notorious for the out-and-out lie. If you have a strong suspicion, the lie can often be made to crumble by applying conditions to it ('If you're so sure, presumably you won't mind a hefty penalty clause') or, at the extreme, walking away.

Other lies are more excusable because the lie applies to the present while the promise is for the future. This sounds more complicated than it is. You are buying a coffee maker for each office in your company. You say to the supplier, 'With an order this big, do you supply a pack of coffee with each machine?' He replies with a straight face, 'Of course'. Technically it's a lie, because he never has before – but he certainly will in your case, so the lie is not disadvantaging you in the negotiation.

The acid test has to be what the impact of the lie is on you, and it is not possible to make hard and fast rules on this. For instance, you could imagine a rule that said 'Anyone who lies about their qualifications is unsuitable for the job'. This would obviously be true if you were negotiating to get a new surgeon for your hospital and a carpenter decided he'd give it a try. On the other hand, if you had a customer-service job to fill and arbitrarily decided that all applicants should have a degree, it's quite likely that the best applicant for the job might not have a degree and might be misleading about it. While you could argue that the sheer act of lying meant the applicant was untrustworthy, it's quite possible that what you've really got is a resourceful person who realizes how unreasonable your criterion is. The point is, though, that the decision has to be made in the individual case – you can't depend on fixed rules.

All this presumes that you can accurately detect a lie, but given that the justice system has never managed to find a way to do this, with all the technology and weight of the law at its disposal, it is highly unlikely that you can always get it right in a negotiation. It could be that the person across the table is simply nervous. The body language of nervousness is close enough to that of lying to make it easy to confuse the two. It could be that each of you is interpreting a statement in a totally different way. Neither of you is lying, but each would find the other's version untrue.

I am not saying that you should tolerate an outrageous lie in negotiation. Nor should you take everything that the other stakeholders say as gospel truth. But the matter of negotiation is largely grey rather than black and white. It does no one any good if you are expecting everything to be a lie, or if you are constantly challenging everyone else's statements. Negotiation often comes down to the old Russian saying that was picked up by the Reagan administration – trust, but verify.

SENSITIVE TO THE MOMENT

However hard you plan, all planning, all strategic consideration is, in the end, guess-work. This is something we don't generally like to hear. A lot of effort frequently goes into planning, and that's fine as long as you accept you are dealing with probabilistic contingencies, rather than what is really going to happen. There is something very irrational about the human brain – once it has a clear picture of how things are going to be, it's a disappointment when things turn out differently. This can happen quite painfully in negotiation.

You reach a point in the discussions where you decided (for instance) that it was appropriate to take a break. But no one wants to. They are really enjoying themselves (it can happen). But it's in the plan, so you insist on the break. The whole impetus is lost and the negotiations collapse. It is crucially important to be aware of your plans, but sensitive to the moment, picking up on the cues that say things are going differently to the way you might have expected.

Often, the most obvious difference between an experienced negotiator and a new-comer is this ability to 'fly by the seat of the pants'. The more your plans are a straitjacket, the less you can make the best out of the negotiation. Plans are there to support you – I'm not suggesting you ignore them – but there are times when you need to ignore the constraints and go with the flow of the discussion.

Probably the hardest aspect of picking up on this advice is deciding when to let go of the plans. After all, they exist for a purpose. There's an interesting parallel in a currently popular TV show that shows families who aren't very good at handling their money how to manage. The presenter insists that the way to shop is to make a list, take just enough cash for the items on that list and don't buy anything else. You can imag-ine the inexperienced shopper going with that intent, but very soon succumbing to the feeling that it's time to let go and BUY. And once again the budget is overspent. However, it might also be that they see a popular, cost-effective household purchase that is two for one at the moment. It isn't on the list. Next week it will be on the list, but it won't be two for one. Now is the time for some discretion, if necessary dropping something else off the list to stick to budget.

Forgive me if I've laboured this point, but it is one that most negotiators often get wrong to start with. Being sensitive to the moment does not mean abandoning your plans. It means being constantly aware of your plans, but when an opportunity arises, as it will, that wasn't catered for, it should be given full consideration. If an opportu-nity arises, it might be worth taking it despite the plans.

Getting this one right will require plenty of mistakes along the way. Like most interpersonal skills, negotiation can rarely be learnt without failure. If you are an inexperienced negotiator, watch how a seasoned professional acts – when he or she sticks to the script, when they go with the moment.

WIDENING THE PICTURE

One of the more interesting aspects of the split between a strategic and a tactical negotiation is the way that one can flow into the other. It may be that the negotiation starts off with the intention of being a one-off transaction, but the variables that are used to manage the negotiation widen the picture, whether they involve taking in different products or services, or going from a single deal to a more strategic agreement.

This often happens in pay negotiations. The employees want more money than the employer intends to put on the table. So the employer widens the picture, moving in the strategic direction. 'I can't give you five per cent now, but we could phase it over the next three years.' Or 'The only way I can afford to give you five per cent is to fix pay at that level for the next four years. It will be tight this year, but I can plan on the basis of no further increases'.

Similarly, a purchasing negotiation might be for a single batch of a consumable product. The buyer says 'I can't afford that, could you drop by 10 per cent?' The seller says 'Not on a one-off sale, my overheads won't take it. But you need widgets every month. If we can agree to a contract for the next three years, I can keep prices down to the level you want. What's more, I can hold them down for the whole period'. A nice example of win–win. The buyer gets a lower price. The vendor gets a cash flow lasting for three years instead of a one-off sale followed by the need to start all over again.

Don't be afraid to widen the picture. Sometimes this can be in a direction that is relatively painless to the stakeholder, but it may still result in big rewards. Publishers usually present authors with contracts specifying a (very small) percentage royalty on each sale. Often authors negotiate for a rising percentage. So after selling (say) 5,000 books, the percentage goes up. The author feels better as there's the possibility of doing better than expected, while the publisher isn't too worried as he or she won't have to pay more unless the book is making a decent profit. A similar approach occurs in any negotiation that results in getting a percentage of the profits of an enterprise as well as a straight fee. It's widening the picture, but in a fail-safe direction.

GETTING TIME RIGHT

Time is always a factor in negotiation: time to plan and prepare in advance of the sessions; managing time in the sessions; the timing of your moves and tactics. How time is employed can often make a big difference. The aggressive negotiator will often use time as a bludgeon, coming up with negotiating stances like, 'I can offer you this very special deal, but you have to make up your mind and agree today. It won't be on the table any longer'.

It is fine to be the one applying time pressure, but being on the receiving end is generally a signal to put the brakes on. If a stakeholder is trying to get you to accept quickly, chances are they have something to hide – they are trying to get you to agree before you can consider all the implications or look more carefully at the alternatives. It is often sensible to say 'I'm sorry, but I really don't understand why this has to be done in such a hurry. If you can't be bothered to wait until we've got everything straight, you obviously don't want to do business'. Effectively calling their bluff, perhaps to the extent of walking away from the table and seeing what happens.

However, a time constraint can sometimes be a legitimate variable to accept. A good example is the process of placing a potential best-selling book with a publisher. Usually, publishing is a buyer's market. The publisher can pick and choose between offerings with little concern if they get it wrong. Occasionally, though, a book comes along that is an obvious best seller. Suddenly it's a seller's market, and the publishers are trying to out do each other to get the book.

In such circumstances, a publisher will sometimes make a pre-emptive bid, saying to the author 'We will give you £X,' where X is perhaps two or three times the amount so far discussed, 'but only if you sign up today'. As always, the negotiator, in this case the author, is taking a risk. He or she may get more elsewhere. There's no knowing how far the bids will go. But equally, they may never get up to this figure, and there's the reassurance that a contract will actually be in place the same day, and the publisher isn't suddenly going to get distracted by another project. It's not an easy call, but the time factor is less of a disaster here.

Slowing things down not only gives time to consider all possibilities and look for potential snares, but can also be beneficial to the emotional side of negotiation. It is all too easy to get carried away with the excitement of negotiation, to lose a temper or to get over-enthusiastic about a doubtful proposition. Time gives the chance to take the edge off the emotional response and mix in the logical. As we will see in the next chapter, good negotiation requires both intuition and logic, but under time pressure, logic is often squeezed out of the equation, resulting in erratic and dangerous decisions.

3

INTUITION VERSUS LOGIC

A BALANCE

As we have already found, a balance between the input of logic and gut feel is essential when negotiating. Dependence on logic alone can result in the sort of out-of-control spirals that happened when share trading was handed over to computers. But shifting entirely to an intuitive, emotional approach brings in decisions that are taken too quickly, without using all the available information appropriately.

This balancing act is not one that stays in constant equilibrium. It has to move with the process. Typically in any creative act there is a repetitive cycle of intuitive opening out followed by logical closing down. Negotiation follows this pattern. Establishing the need for negotiation in the first place may involve some gut feeling, but then it's down to the logic of preparation (perhaps inspired by a little intuition to know where to probe for possible unexpected turns in the negotiation).

Around the negotiating table there is a constant pulse between the inevitable gut-feel responses and the checking balance of information. Opening up new avenues involves intuitive creativity; coming down to an agreed point often requires a logical focus. Developing the skills to be a good negotiator requires an unusually strong balance between the two. That is why you will find a whole list of different topics for further reading in Chapter 6. In negotiating you need to know people and creativity. You need to understand motivation and be able to manage time. You need to cope with stress and be able to ferret out appropriate information. The great negotiator is a modern-day renaissance person.

USING EMOTION

Emotion inevitably enters into negotiations. Any interaction between people will be flavoured by emotion, and the intuition and gut feel that is a vital part of negotiation is impossible without it. The negotiator's aim has to be to use emotion effectively without being controlled by it. As soon as you lose your temper, you have given away control of the negotiation. However, you can use the whole gamut of emotion – from anger to joy – to put across your message and reinforce your position.

Exactly how emotion is employed in negotiations depends very much on the people involved. There are individual variations, but also cultural inclinations. Some cultures consider a vivid display of emotion such a normal part of everyday life that they would think that a negotiator who didn't show emotion regularly had something to hide. Other cultures consider shows of emotion in business a sign of weakness. If you are to use emotion effectively, part of your preparation needs to be finding out as much as you can about the other stakeholders in the negotiation, establishing their personal and cultural attitudes.

The emotions that are most frequently and safely employed in most Western negotiations are anger and friendliness. Anger has to be used sparingly, and almost artificially.

It's fine to appear angry and even to feel some anger, as long as you haven't lost control to the anger. Anger is best employed to counter an outrageous suggestion from the other side, and can be most effective if it very quickly turns into sorrow with them thinking that they can treat you in this way.

Usually, though, there is most leverage from warmth and friendship. The more you can put this across, the harder it will be for the other stakeholders to comprehensively rip you off. To get the value out of warmth and friendship you will need to maximize the human contact between the parties. This is why it is always best that at least part of the negotiation takes place face to face. You can do plenty over the phone or by e-mail, but these remote communications lack the emotional linkage. It's much easier to stop thinking of someone as a person if you haven't had a face-to-face meeting with them lately, and this, in turn, is a disadvantage to someone when you don't think of them as a person.

Even high-quality video conferencing lacks this warmth factor. You may be able to see and talk to the other stakeholders with perfect quality, but you can't build the same level of social bonding. Opportunities to meet socially, to discuss things other than the negotiation, to regard the other stakeholders as acquaintances and even friends, all increase the chances of getting warmth into the equation.

But, like the anger, can't you fake it? Not so easily. A short burst of anger is relatively easy to generate, but faked warmth is usually easily detected – and dangerously off-putting. By far the easiest way to fake warmth is to actually feel it, to think of the other stakeholders as real people and to like them for their humanity. For all but the most consummate actors, finding something to like about almost anyone else is easier than generating a convincing fake.

The objective of projecting warmth is mostly to generate reciprocal feeling. It's hard not to be nicer to someone you feel is being nice to you. We all crave affection, however shallow. It's much easier to line yourself up with the beliefs of someone you like. In effect, that warmth is softening up the other stakeholders, making them easier to move. It's a vital emotion.

DEALING WITH PEOPLE

I can't reiterate enough that negotiations are human relations, with all the flaws and difficulties (and fun) that accompany all human relations. I was speaking recently to the director of a major financial institution. He had been involved with merger negotiations with another large institution, this time Swiss. By mid-afternoon on the first day, things were going well, but were tense. The Swiss negotiators wanted a coffee break. The other stakeholders wanted to continue. For a period the negotiation nearly fell through. The Swiss negotiators were prepared to drop a whole multi-billion dollar deal over a cup of coffee. That's people for you.

It's all very well to say that negotiation requires you to balance logic and gut feel, but sometimes human nature introduces a third factor that is neither of these – sheer bloody-mindedness. Everyone has moments when they operate irrationally, over-reacting to a stimulus or being ridiculously intransigent. In such circumstances, an understanding of human nature and a willingness to work around it are essential.

The natural reaction when someone else goes into extreme irrationality is to follow them. When they insult your family, you insult theirs. When they threaten to walk out, so do you. But the good negotiator is enough in control to be able to handle over-reaction and irrationality calmly, bringing the negotiation back on track. You have to be prepared to apologize, overcoming pride when you know you have done nothing wrong. Often, the over-reaction will have been triggered by misunderstanding. Calmly and slowly point out what was really intended. Verbally sympathize with their view-point, even if you don't inside. Until the stakeholders can be brought back out of irrationality, no progress can be made.

Often such over-reaction is simply human nature, but occasionally it will be cyni-cally used as a bargaining counter, with the intention that you give way on some issue in order to stop the irrationality. It's a classic child's technique, that all too often works for children so that the adults can get a bit of peace. While it is important to soothe the other stakeholders, it is equally important to totally ignore any conditions they are putting on their return to normal. Keep assuring them there was no bad intention and apologizing for any misunderstanding, without ever moving an inch on any conces-sions. There is a limit to how long any over-reaction can be sustained in the face of sympathy (although it can totally finish negotiations if you over-react back). Before long, with no concessions required, the other stakeholders will pull back to normality.

CULTURE SHOCK

Time and again, cultural differences have caused problems in negotiations. Anything from how the other stakeholders are addressed to how much price haggling is allowed and expected will have cultural variants. Like the over-reaction in the section above, such cultural upsets are sometimes used as a cynical bargaining chip, but often arouse genuine upset in the parties to a negotiation and so disrupt the whole process.

Cultural differences will bring in different expectations, difficulties in communica-tion and differences in attitude to timing. It might be, for instance, that representatives of two cultures are meeting for the first time for a social event on the evening before a formal negotiation. One culture might expect to have early discussions on the subject of the negotiation. The other might expect to stick to social niceties. This second group would find the first pushy, while the first would find their opponents evasive. Neither is doing anything wrong, apart from not anticipating the other's cultural reac-tion.

It's a good thing before a negotiation with a different culture to immerse yourself as much as possible in their tradition. Talk to other people who have already dealt with them. Read up on the culture. Talk to a friendly person from the same culture. Try to get a picture of how they are likely to react to something and why.

Sometimes taking such care can result in amusing circumstances. After all, you aren't necessarily the only one who has done their homework for the occasion. A famous example was the first meeting of IBM and Apple to discuss a new business venture. These two companies might have been from the same country, but their cultures were poles apart. IBM was all East Coast, button-down formality; Apple was West Coast, beard and sandals openness. Each did their homework. So at the first meeting the Apple folk turned up wearing suits and white shirts. The IBM team were in jeans and T-shirts. Each had made an effort to match the other's culture. Despite the apparent failure of both teams to achieve a cultural match, the result was positive. Each was impressed by the other's attempt. The very humour of the situation helped to break down barriers. Negotiations went a great deal better thanks to this confusion.

Like many human issues, once you have established a basic level of trust between stakeholders, it makes a great deal of sense to get the issue out into the open. If there are aspects of the behaviour of the other team that you don't understand, ask them about it. Not in a derogatory way, but with a genuine interest. If, for instance, you found that a Spanish negotiator never turned up until mid-afternoon for the lunchtime session, you might be irritated at his recurrent lateness. Berate him about this, and the whole negotiation would probably collapse. But ask him about it in a positive way and he will be happy to let you know that he can only work in the afternoon after a siesta – and you, no doubt, will cease to be irritated and be happy to accommodate him.

TYPE PROFILES AND HOROSCOPES

The problems arising from differences among cultures also crop up in negotiations between different types of individual. Jungian psychology recognizes a number of personality types. You might, for instance, be more extrovert or introvert, more inclined to think or feel, more likely to be judgemental or perceptive. A number of methods exist, among the best known are the Myers-Briggs Type Profile and the Insights Colour Wheel, to classify individuals according to the personality traits that are strongest in them.

Just taken on its own, this seems to have little more value than horoscopes, although with the big advantage that a type profile identifies what you are from how you respond, rather than when you were born. But the power of such indicators is the ability to recognize that someone else has different traits, and that they are irritating you not out of bloody-mindedness, but because they see the world in a different way.

If you know the type profiles of the participants in a negotiation, it is much easier to understand that they are behaving in a particular way because that's how they naturally react. However, many people don't know their own type profiles, and it may not be convenient to test them as part of the negotiation.

You can, however, still be aware of the types of behaviour that are typical as a result of different type profiles, and to be wary of your own natural response to these. Such awareness can make all the difference. For instance, some people are natural Pareto people. They want to do the 20 per cent of the work that gives 80 per cent of the result, then move on to something else. Other people like to make sure every last detail is correct. The Pareto people can have a prodigious output, performing as if they were several normal people. Their natural response to the perfectionist is impatience. They will keep checking to see if everything is finished, desperately wanting to get on to the next challenge. By contrast, the perfectionist will have a much smaller output, but each product of their labour will be superbly crafted. The perfectionist will find the Pareto person's constant nagging a huge irritation, and can be appalled at the gaps in their work.

There is nothing wrong with either approach (provided the Pareto person does actually achieve the 80 per cent level, and provided the perfectionist ever finishes anything at all). But, unless these people understand and accept the nature of the other, each will find the other's behaviour extremely irritating. The first stage in coping with personality differences is to accept that there are different behaviours, and that all are equally valid. Some may be more appropriate than others for different aspects of a negotiation, but all are valid.

The second stage of coping is to communicate. For instance, the Pareto person is not a stickler for rules, but likes to get things finished and move on. It is in his or her nature to say 'Right, have we got that finished, so we can move on?' At regular intervals, such a personality will expect to be told about progress, or will pester others until they get an update. The perfectionist may have a view of 'It takes as long as it takes', and finds each request for an update an increasing irritation. In the second stage, the Pareto person could explain that there is no intention of curtailing the perfectionist's skills, and they are free to take as long as they like. But the Pareto person has a need to keep on top of progress, so could they agree to have regular updates at a specified interval, then there will be no more pestering. Or whatever.

The final stage of coping is to implement the procedure with whoever's temperament is best suited to it driving the process. In this example, it is liable to be the Pareto person who keeps track of the milestones (although there are other personality types even better suited to this) and flags them up to the perfectionist – but not in the form of a threat.

Pareto and perfectionist are but two types in a spectrum, and indicators like Myers-Briggs typically recognize 16 different types. It's neither practical to identify them all here, nor even necessary. The point is, rather, that when someone else's behaviour in negotiation is irritating you, it's important to establish what is happening and how and why you differ, then to communicate this difference so that you can manage it between you.

DEALING WITH STRESS

Stress is a fact of life, whatever your occupation, but there is something particularly stressful about negotiation. It's the combination of the natural human relationship with the constraints and deviousness of negotiation that seems to pile on the stress. Of itself, stress isn't always a bad thing. It is only through a degree of stress that it is possible to go the extra mile and win over the odds. But too prolonged an exposure to stress is a killer.

At the heart of stress is control. You might have vast amounts of things to do, huge mountains to climb, but as long as you are in control, there doesn't have to be much stress involved. When you lose control, though, whether it's to other people, to the system or to time, stress can get ugly.

Responding to stress is a combination of prevention and cure. The time component, for instance, can be helped immensely by the often underrated skill of time management. Some stresses originating from a system can rarely be managed away, unless you get out of the system entirely. In these cases, it is more effective to apply a physical, mental or spiritual salve to the stress. It might be deep breathing or massage, boosting your self-esteem or having a spiritual anchor. Whatever the source, something can be done about stress.

A lot of the stresses in negotiating come from the feeling that you are out of control. Establishing control of the negotiation can make all the difference. Negotiation doesn't have to be stressful – it can even be fun in the right circumstances – but you should be able to manage your own stress levels to cope, even if you can't remove the stress. In this book we will touch on stress management, but it is a major subject in its own right. See page 129 of Chapter 6 for further reading on stress.

BUILDING TRUST

Trust is an essential for effective negotiation. In negotiations without trust, the stakeholders are like fighters, circling each other looking for advantage, never daring to turn their backs in case they are attacked when they aren't looking. The fundamental requirement needed to be able to establish a win–win outcome is a degree of trust.

You can help your chances of successful negotiation by making it easier for the other stakeholders to trust you. It's a peculiarity of trust that it is much more dependent on what you do than on what you say. It doesn't matter how wonderful you are when speaking, if you act differently there can be no trust. 'Do what I say, not what I do' is not an acceptable motto for a negotiator.

Why are actions so important? Because as soon as you say one thing and do another, the other stakeholders are going to think 'It doesn't matter what he says, he's going to do something different'. And the whole basis of negotiation is talking in order to establish what will be done in the future. If, on the other hand, the other stakeholders think 'I can always rely on her to do what she says she's going to do', they will feel more open to discuss things with you. They will accept your word on the way things are. And the negotiations can proceed.

If you have a long-term relationship with the other stakeholders, that trust might be there from the start. In many cases, though, you have to build trust. This is another reason why you might feel it helpful to slow down a negotiation. Trust takes time to grow. You need to be able to demonstrate that you can follow words with action; not necessarily in this specific negotiation, but in general. Trust will follow.

A LITTLE ENDORSEMENT

If you need to build trust relatively quickly, the normal approach is to use endorsement. It's a term that has become sadly devalued thanks to the advertisers' use of endorsements by famous people as a way of selling products. Cynically, we know that the famous athlete who is raving about the sports drink probably can't stand the stuff, but is being paid enough to say anything. This isn't endorsement, it's prostitution. But true endorsement still has a value.

If you are negotiating to sell your services, it can be very helpful in building trust if you can have satisfied customers to tell your potential buyer just how great you have been. Sometimes, you can get a professional endorser, whose own standing depends on the objectiveness of his or her input. This could be anything from a journalist reviewing your product to a surveyor giving a house the seal of approval as safe to buy. Too often, we are embarrassed at the thought of seeking out endorsement – we don't like asking other people to praise us. Yet this is a hugely valuable tool in building trust in the artificial confines of the negotiation. Whatever your negotiation, look for the opportunity to make honest use of endorsement.

EVALUATING OPTIONS

Variables are wonderful things. When you are negotiating a deal, you can always throw in another variable to give an extra edge to your pitch. But both sides of the negotiation have access to variables, and the impact of a range of variables on the decision-making process can be to cause confusion. Sometimes this is done intentionally. It's hard to believe, for example, that the PCs you see on offer from various suppliers aren't in such a bewildering array of configurations and bundles just so that it's impossible to compare like with like. Before you reach a decision you are going to need to use gut feel, but first should come some form of logical evaluation.

It's a common enough predicament. There are a number of options to choose between. The problem is to know which one to go with. It's equally true of negotiating a deal, choosing where to go for lunch or deciding who to hire for a job. Evaluating options isn't particularly glamorous, but without it your negotiations will not deliver the best results. Because there is often a degree of calculation involved, it's the sort of thing that is best handled offline if possible.

Before you plunge into evaluation, you need to be sure of your criteria. What will you use to decide which option is best? For instance, if you were buying a car, you might look at criteria like price, comfort, speed, appearance, and so on. In a negotiation, you may well have identified many of the criteria – as most variables will provide criteria for choice – but don't assume that the variables you are working with are necessarily all the criteria. Explore the options first.

Given the criteria, you then need some means of scoring the different options against them. With a numerical factor like price, this is easy. With something less quantifiable like 'level of customer service' or 'quality', you may not actually have numbers. It makes things easier to work with if you can use a numerical scale to rate the different options with (say) 10 as best and 0 as worst.

You can then use a little simple arithmetic to combine the criteria scores and get an idea of how your different options pan out. Of course, you will have to make sure that the criteria are all working on the same scale. If, for instance, you have used a 0–10 scale for qualitative criteria, you will need to factor a criterion like price, so it worked on the same scale. Note also that some criteria (again like price) are actually negative – the bigger they are the worse they are.

That's not all you can do, though. It's almost always the case that some criteria are more important to a decision than others. To cope with this you can apply weightings. For instance, if you decided that on-time delivery was twice as important as delivering beyond your base country, you could halve all the scores for the second criterion.

With these figures, a spreadsheet and a bit of head scratching you can come up with a result, prioritizing the options. But be careful, dangers lurk among the numbers. Even if you get everything right, the combinatorial explosion means that if you have more than a few options and a few criteria, you could spend all day inputting values. It's much better to take a first pass and weed out the obvious insignificant options and criteria so you have less to deal with.

A more insidious problem is when the numbers go wrong. It could be simple arithmetical problems, but it could also be a matter of scales. If you make sure that for each criterion the top selection scores (say) 10, then the weightings will make sense, but if each scale has an arbitrary top number you can't combine them.

While you can do this sort of thing with a spreadsheet, look out for specialist software to help, as the real benefit of taking this approach results not from just getting a result (option X is better), but from being able to play tunes on the data (what would happen if…). The aim of this option evaluation process is not to fix the way you want the negotiation to go, but to better understand the options and criteria. One reason you certainly aren't going to come up with a definitive answer is that there is always room for gut feel.

GOING WITH THE GUT

In fact, whatever the numbers say, it is your intuition that is going to drive the final decision of how to play things. Not only do you not have time to mess about with numbers too much around the negotiating table, it's also true that decisions have to be made with a human component to be most flexible and effective. One of the option evaluation software packages I use (see **www.cul.co.uk/software** for more detail) allows you to perform an option evaluation, then see how much you will have to change the variables to get the option you want rather than the logical outcome. This can be immensely valuable in understanding just what is happening in the decision-making process.

I am not criticizing information here. It is vital to have the right information available before handling the decision-making process, but in the end the decision needs to be in the hands of experience and gut feel.

That's a pragmatic fact – it's what works best – but what is really happening? In all the studies of knowledge management it has been established that knowledge is a hybrid thing. No matter how much you try to stuff knowledge into a computer, you still need a human expert to interpret the information and the situation and to creatively apply what he or she knows to the requirement. Knowledge without this human input quickly becomes out of date, and can only be applied to a small range of problems near the situations that generated the original knowledge. The more there is change and extrapolation, the more the human component is needed.

And that's exactly what is happening in a negotiation. What we describe as gut feel is really the human capability to take a whole bunch of information, combine it with the current situation, extrapolate possible outcomes and go for the best option with what is known. At risk of using a word that has been devalued by overuse, this is truly an awesome capability.

4

PROCESS VERSUS COMMUNICATIONS

THE BALANCE

Every aspect of negotiation falls somewhere on the spectrum from process to human communication. Many factors and techniques combine the two, but some sit at different ends of the range. A good negotiator needs to establish skills in handling both process and communication. In a broad sense, all the process aspects could be handled by the negotiator alone, although often they may stretch into the negotiation itself. By definition, the communication aspects must involve someone else.

In this chapter we will briefly explore a sandwich of process and communications. The filling is the pure communication – talking and listening, the nature of assertiveness. At the far end come the more strategic process aspects around setting a direction and keeping track of the process. But we will begin with the process elements that are most closely associated with negotiation, the tactical detail, starting with that most interesting of subjects: the price.

THE MATTER OF PRICE

You can't talk about selling for long before price comes up. It would be very strange if this wasn't the case. Yet the first consideration when dealing with price is to make sure that it isn't over-valued. Yes, it is important, but it shouldn't always dominate a negotiation. Instead, price should be seen alongside a whole host of other variables (see the next section). It's only in context that it is meaningful. Take a simple example: you are buying computer printers for your company. One supplier offers a unit price of £200, another £120. Which do you go with?

The answer should be, 'I don't know, there's insufficient information'. For instance, you may be waiting for me to tell you that the annual consumables cost of the first printer is £100 and the second is £200. And so on. Yes, price is important, but it is usually so visible (and we are often so fixed on the short-term view) that it sometimes is given excessive importance.

If you are selling, there always comes that uncomfortable moment when you've got to set a price. From the strategy section, you will already have an idea of what you want and need to get. Setting that initial price on paper is a good idea – a price list gives a false air of officialdom to a price. The level needs to be pitched so that it is not outrageously high in market terms, but not so low you haven't room to be still comfortable after manoeuvre.

I have seen it suggested that you should avoid round number prices (like £10, £100 or £1400), because this suggests a starting price for negotiation. Apart from the fact that this is what your price is likely to be, I'm not totally convinced about this argument. There's some justification for using the standing retail trick of £399.95 instead of £400, but I'm not sure if £403 is really somehow better that £400, too.

When you have to lower a price as a seller, make sure it's in decreasing increments, making it harder and harder to get too far down, emphasizing that you are running out of space to move. One piece of advice I would certainly follow – never give anything away (on price or any other variable), wait for them to ask (and don't be too quick to accept). In fact silence is often an underrated negotiating skill. You can often get people to negotiate themselves down, given enough silence.

THERE'S ALWAYS ANOTHER LEVER

As we've already seen, price is but one of a huge host of variables. Here's a representative sample in no particular order:

- Maintenance cost.
- Consumable cost.
- Delivery charges.
- Delivery time.
- Expenses.
- Materials.
- Finance.
- Guarantees and warranties.
- Product quality.
- Packaging.
- Bulk discount.
- Delayed payment.
... and so on.

If you are in trouble in a negotiation and don't have the leeway to move on a particular variable, remember just how many other options there are. If the other stakeholder points out that you are 10 per cent more expensive than your rival, you can argue 'Yes, but we can deliver in a week to their month, and you don't have to pay a penny with us until the Summer'. Or whatever.

YOUR USP

In sales and marketing there is one acronym that is engraved on everyone's heart – USP. The Unique Selling Proposition is something almost every company could make more of than it does at the moment. It's what's special about your product, your services, your business, your people that makes them different from the rest. A good USP is simple, readily understood by the employees and readily understood by the customers. An old, but well known one is the John Lewis Partnership's 'Never knowingly undersold'.

Unfortunately, USPs do get out of date and devalued. 'Never knowingly undersold' is something many companies could say nowadays, and it's arguable that John Lewis would be better working on quality and service lines. However, the point is still that a USP makes a lot of difference when selling.

When you are negotiating, your USP should be to the fore. If, for example, you were in a business where support generally operated in office hours and you had 24-hour support, it should be something that was worked into your negotiations as strongly as possible, in many different ways. Your USP should be a prime tool in selling your side of the negotiation, provided it is strong enough. Just make sure it truly is unique.

LISTENING

I had initially intended 'listening' to come after the next section 'talking' – but that would be getting things back to front. Good communication (good negotiating) starts with listening. The fact is that most of us are pretty good at talking, but hopeless at listening. We tend to spend the time when others are talking getting ready for our next bit of speech, half-listening, with most of our conscious mind working out the clever things that we are going to say.

This makes for bad communication, because it's usually quite clear that you aren't giving full attention, and it makes for bad negotiation because it's all too easy to miss a critical point. If, when you are listening, something occurs to you, make a quick note, don't keep worrying at it in your mind. If necessary, get the speaker to reiterate to make sure you don't lose track. But when you are listening, do just that. Listen. Take in what they are saying. Make a note of anything this makes you think of, but stick with the plot.

Just by listening, really listening, you will have put yourself ahead of the majority of negotiators. You will have won more trust from the other stakeholders – because you were obviously really interested in what they were saying – and you will have a grasp of exactly what they are saying, not a vague overview, with the gaps filled in by your imagination.

TALKING

Talking is equally at the heart of negotiation. Whether you are selling or exploring, talking is a fundamental. It might seem that talking is something that can be left to nature, that it's something everyone can do, but the way that you handle your input can be crucial. The aim should be to be relaxed, whatever the pressures, to be positive and to be fluent. There is nothing that will beat practice in this field. Especially bearing in mind the need from the previous section to listen to the other parties, you have to be able to spring into speech with very little thinking time.

Don't take this as an excuse for waffling. Give yourself a second or two to collect your thoughts. A useful approach if you feel you aren't sure where to start is to try to pull together what has already been said. Echo back what you have heard from the other parties – make sure there is clear understanding. And make appropriate use of notes (see *Taking notes*, 5.2) to ensure that you have a range of openings available to you. Most of all, a negotiator needs to be able to engage his or her brain before speaking, sadly a rare ability. Before undertaking negotiation for real, get some practice in. Undertake some mock negotiations with your colleagues. It doesn't matter how much you read up and learn valuable techniques, your communication skills will benefit most of all from being used.

An important tool in the talking side of negotiation is silence. It's frighteningly powerful. Silence can force the other parties to expand on their statements, and sometimes to modify them as they realize that they are inappropriate. Silence can be overused – you will just appear inarticulate – but as a reaction to an incomplete or dubious statement, silence can be devastating. Use your face to complement the silence. Practise with a mirror. You don't want to be mugging like a ham actor, but a slight raise of the eyebrow, a quizzical concern, a tilt of the head can all help to reinforce the power of silence as a lever.

ASSERTIVE OR AGGRESSIVE?

Aggression in a negotiation will not lead to a win–win outcome. In those rare circumstances where you are sure this isn't required, you may feel that you can afford to be aggressive, but even there it's not the right answer. The trouble with aggression is that it kicks in the ancient fight or flight response. The other stakeholders will have no choice but to respond as they are programmed. They will either run away or fight back. Running away could mean literally leaving the negotiating table or finding ways to avoid discussion. Fighting back could be anything from getting aggressive in their turn to physical violence. None of these responses will help to conclude the negotiation.

But curbing aggression does not mean that you are going to be a wimp and give in to whatever the other stakeholders want. The appropriate position is to be assertive, but not aggressive. It's rather unfortunate that being assertive has been taken on as one of the clarion cries of some fringe groups – it somehow seems to fit with self-defence and holistic medicine. This misses the point. Being assertive is simply a matter of ensuring that your viewpoint is heard and that you get an appropriate chance to get your way without being aggressive.

The first and most important aid to being assertive rather than aggressive is to be calm. Nothing can be more unnerving than appropriately applied calm. It might be hard to stay calm sometimes, when tempers are fraying and the other stakeholders are being unreasonable or abusive, but calm will do you a lot more good than anger. By staying calm, you appear to be in the right (whether or not you are). By staying calm you can help to defuse the situation. And by staying calm you will not say things that you (and your negotiation) might regret.

Achieving calm under pressure is not always easy. One of the reasons you will find a number of techniques and whole a list of books in Chapter 6 on stress management is that negotiations are stressful, and you often need help to stay calm. A simple breathing exercise can make all the difference. Psychologically you can also help yourself to stay calm by keeping everything in proportion. Most negotiations are not earth-shattering. The world will still turn, the sun will still rise, whatever the outcome. So why are you getting into such a state?

With calm as a foundation you can build up assertiveness. The essential is to get your point across, whatever the opposition, in a calm and positive way. This may mean repeating yourself – the oldest assertiveness technique in the book is the broken record, where you repeat what you want over and over again, whatever the response, until the other person gives in. It may involve breaking into the flow of other stakeholders who always want to get their point in rather than yours.

If you want your point to be heard, it's a good idea not to put the other stakeholders' backs up by disagreeing. If you launch in with 'I see what you are saying, but...' they have already switched off. You are contradicting them and they won't like it. Much better to appear to build on what they are saying, even if you are in total disagreement. Saying instead something like 'I understand your point of view, and we could...' is much more likely to get your side of the argument across because you are being inclusive ('we could') and you have used 'and' instead of 'but', making your statement seem a constructive addition rather than an argument.

It might seem that such picky concentration on words is irrelevant to getting a result, but such words set the tone of the negotiation. The more you can seem positive and agreeable, even if your remarks are in total contradiction, the harder it will be to dismiss what you are saying.

A final thought on being assertive – have plenty of supporting material. It is much easier to stay assertive if you can cite all sorts of examples and endorsements for your point of view. That way, you aren't just saying 'This is the way things should be because I say so', which can slip easily from being assertive to being just bossy. Exuding calm, staying positive, reiterating your point and using plenty of supporting material – being assertive won't guarantee a result, but it will maximize your chances of success.

ESTABLISHING A DIRECTION

Sometimes, particularly where a negotiation is about fact finding rather than selling, it isn't clear at the start just where you are going. If so, take time out from the negotiation to establish goals. Without them it is as if you were wandering lost without a map in trackless wastes. Be explicit about this. Don't try to work it into the general discussion; say that you feel there's a need to be clear about the goals of the negotiation, and spend a little time establishing them.

A number of creativity techniques can be useful here. Get an overview of the background to your discussions. Pool your information and have the people who know it best give you a guided tour. Then have a shot at putting together a statement of intent – what it is that you are attempting to do. Finally, test that statement.

One technique that is very effective in doing this is to ask 'why' repeatedly. For instance, if you said your negotiation was to agree the best way to roster staff to cover your schedule of trains, you might ask 'Why do want to roster staff to cover your train schedule?' The answer might be 'To make sure the trains run on time'. And so 'Why do you want the trains to run on time?' That might be 'To make our passengers happier with the service'. The answer to why this time might be 'To keep the passengers', or 'To keep our operating licence' or 'To increase profits', and so on.

When you have used this repeated 'why' technique, you will have a number of statements that could themselves be a basis for negotiation. Agreeing how to make the trains run on time, or how to make the passengers happier, for instance. This exercise enables you to question the intent of the negotiation and devise alternative goals.

A second approach that can be valuable is to look for obstacles. What makes the negotiation necessary? Why can't you just go ahead and do whatever is required? The removal of these obstacles could become the goals of the negotiation.

It may be that you know right from the start exactly what the negotiation is about, and that's fine. But all too often you start with an unclear picture, or you are trying to deal with symptoms rather than causes, and taking a little time to clarify the goals will make the whole process of negotiation more practical.

PLOTTING OUT THE JOURNEY

As you undertake a negotiation, change is always occurring. Unless there is movement, as we have already seen, there is no successful negotiation. However, in a complex deal it is very easy to lose track of the different variables and the state of play. It can be useful to have some sort of record of the situation, making it clear just where you have got to, particularly in an exploratory negotiation.

In such circumstances, consider having a large whiteboard or similar vehicle, showing the state of play. You may find that a diagram (see *Taking notes*, 5.2) might be most effective in clarifying the position – but whatever means you use, keep the situation visible. Apart from anything else, this frees up mental resources in the negotiators that would otherwise be taken up with remembering what has happened so far. Whether you are exploring or selling, you want the negotiation to come to a conclusion; without an end, it will have been a total waste of time. Plotting out the journey you have taken will make it easier to reach a conclusion.

5

THE EXERCISES

5.1 | *Lifetime value*

Preparation None.
Running time Five minutes.
Resources Company information.
Timing Once.

Identify your company's top three customers. It should be possible to find out who they are – however big your company, this is the sort of information you ought to know. Work out, in round figures, their lifetime value to the company. That is the amount they are worth to you each year multiplied by the number of years you expect to do business with them.

Feedback   Think of your overall value for the lifetime of the relationship to the other stakeholders in a negotiation – and their value to you. Think also of the lifetime impact of your negotiation on that relationship. Some aspects of lifetime value are easier to calculate than others. It's easy for a supplier to get a ballpark figure for a customer. It's harder to establish a supplier's lifetime value to you. One contributing factor is any benefits gained from the supplier's products, plus the particular impact of the unique reasons why you should go for that supplier and not some other (the supplier should be happy to provide these).

Other negotiations may be even harder to get into this mindset – but try anyway. For instance, in a union negotiation, it's fairly easy to see the lifetime value of the relationship of worker and company both ways if you think about it. Whatever the negotiation, lifetime value is worth thinking of. It needn't take long. This is a crude approximation for guidance, not an accountant's forecast. A high lifetime value for a stakeholder may make you prepared to go for a loss leader, and to make sure that the stakeholder is given the impression that you care very much about them. Even 'small' customers can have a considerable lifetime value. Supermarkets, for instance, might be less cavalier about doing deals with individual customers if they considered that a typical family lifetime value could easily be over £100,000.

Outcome   Lifetime value is an extremely valuable tool when assessing how much weight to put on strategic and tactical considerations in a negotiation.

Variations   None.

Strategic	✪✪✪✪
Intuitive	✪
Process	✪✪✪✪
Fun	✪✪

5.2 | *Taking notes*

Preparation None.
Running time 20 minutes.
Resources Pen and paper.
Timing Several times.

Note taking is an essential skill in managing a negotiation. You need to be able to take notes while keeping most of your attention focussed on the discussion. Even more importantly, you need to be able to find a note without losing concentration. Graphical notes are ideal for this requirement. In this exercise, take about 20 minutes to make graphical notes of the main points you know about negotiating.

Start at the centre of a page or whiteboard and draw an image that represents the core of the issue. From this, radiate out branches that represent the major themes of the issue. From each of these draw progressively lower and lower level themes.

On each of the branches write one or two keywords above the line to say what that issue is. For instance, one branch might be profit, splitting into costs and revenues, with revenues splitting into direct sales and indirect and costs splitting into the major cost drivers.

In general, try to make the image organic. Start with larger and fatter branches at the centre, moving to smaller and smaller ones and eventually twigs at the extremities. You might also use different colours for each major branch (and make all subsidiaries the same colour as the major branch).

Feedback Note taking while keeping focus improves with practice. This exercise is a one-off one in terms of learning the basics of visual note taking, but should be repeated by putting the technique into use. Every time you go to a meeting, try taking notes this way (whether or not you need any) as practice.

Outcome Better note taking will result in staying on top of the negotiation and being able to respond instantly to any opportunity. It's a must.

Variations There are various alternative note-taking strategies but none can compare with this approach for negotiations. See details of *Instant Brainpower* and *The Mind Map Book* in Chapter 6 (page 124) for more on effective note taking.

Strategic ✪
Intuitive ✪✪
Process ✪✪✪✪
Fun ✪✪✪

5.3 | **Web research**

Preparation Familiarize yourself with Internet mining.
Running time 30 minutes.
Resources Web access.
Timing Once.

The World Wide Web, and to some extent other aspects of the Internet, offers a whole new resource for finding out more about the other stakeholders in a negotiation and what their starting position will be.

Pick a large company that you might need to do business with in the future, and also a key individual in that company. Check out the company and the individual in a range of search engines. Use business information sources to get more detail on what the company is up to. If you've time in the exercise (you would certainly do this in a real negotiation), don't stick to the single company. Look at its competitors and suppliers as well.

Feedback There has never been so much information so readily available as is now the case through the Web. If you aren't familiar with the skills required to get the best out of the Web, see the section on Research books in Chapter 6 (page 125). To get a taster of some of the potential sources of information, see the Web site accompanying the book *Mining the Internet* at **http://www.cul.co.uk/mining**.

Initially, there was another section on researching the other stakeholders by conventional means, but I realized that there wasn't much left to put in it. Yes, you might use (say) the *Wall Street Journal* – but the easiest way to get to it is via the Internet. Of course, there is still conventional research to be done, but it's very much the mechanism to fill in the gaps, no longer the primary approach.

Outcome There is no doubt that information is vital to negotiation, whatever the style or importance of the exercise. To ignore the power of the Internet in this respect would be to waste a massive resource.

Variations None.

Strategic	✪✪✪✪
Intuitive	✪
Process	✪✪✪✪
Fun	✪✪✪

5.4 | *The agreement space*

Preparation None.
Running time 15 minutes.
Resources Pen and paper.
Timing Once.

Before undertaking a significant negotiation it is a good idea to plot out the space in which the negotiating variables lie. On a sheet of paper, draw up a 2-axis chart with a diagonal line at 45 degrees. Something like this:

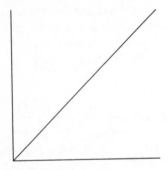

Make the vertical axis cost and the horizontal axis value (if you are selling, the cost will be to the stakeholder, the benefit to you; if you are buying, it's the other way around). Now plot each of the variables on the chart. You could use a point with a label or just a letter or symbol.

This chart will give you a good feel for the leverage any particular variable has. If it is high cost and low value, it will be of limited use in the negotiation. Some variables (typically price) will come around the diagonal, with cost and value roughly equal. Most interestingly, some will fall in the bottom right-hand side, where the cost is low but the value is high. These are the variables needed really to achieve movement. Cherish them.

Feedback As an exercise, try this out for a fictional negotiation (or even better, a historical negotiation), to get a feel for what you need to know about the variables and for using the plot. Note *Another lever*, 5.25, when undertaking this exercise. Once you have got your plot together, look for other possible variables that you could bring into the equation.

You may doubt the existence of variables with low cost and high value – they tend to be the ones with a large markup, or a high development cost followed by a very low unit cost, or involve trading a valuable product or service that is unlikely to be cashed in. Good examples would be money-back guarantees, competitions and two-for-one offers on low production cost products like CDs.

Outcome   An understanding of the leverage each variable can exert on the negotiation, and hence of the best tactics to use in employing them.

Variations   None.

Strategic ✪✪✪
Intuitive ✪
Process ✪✪✪✪
Fun ✪✪

5.5 | *Hearing what they really say*

Preparation None.
Running time 10 minutes.
Resources None.
Timing Several times.

Listening is a prime tool for the negotiator, but all too often we are too busy preparing what we are going to say next to give more than half an ear to what is being said. This is fatal in negotiation.

Take the opportunity in the next few meetings you are involved in to drop out of active mode for 10 minutes. Don't get ready to throw your bit in, just listen. Really listen. If you feel a response bubbling up, scribble it down on a piece of paper and forget it until your listening time is up. Don't just listen to the words, listen to how they are said, what non-verbal communication accompanies them. Try to put what you are hearing into context, building up a mental picture of the situation.

Feedback Listening like this takes practice, but unless you force yourself to really listen and not think of a response (and avoid planning your weekend trip) you will not get the most out of a negotiation. It will probably help to focus your listening if you take notes. See *Taking notes*, 5.2 for a way to make sure your note taking is effective.

Outcome Listening well is the hardest part of communicating. Unless you listen well your communications will suffer, and so will your negotiation.

Variations Try your listening skills in a wide range of different environments and with different distractions. How well do you manage when several people are trying to get their point across at once, or when there are visual distractions? Don't expect overnight change. Although each individual exercise can be short, building listening skills is a long-term course of development.

Strategic ✪
Intuitive ✪✪✪
Process ✪
Fun ✪✪

5.6 | *Are they telling the truth?*

Preparation None.
Running time Five minutes.
Resources None.
Timing Once.

In each of the examples below, take a couple of moments to see how you would react before reading the feedback. Next time you are really negotiating, or just talking with other people, be on the lookout for the suspicion of untruth and try to be more analytical in your response. Everyone can manage detachment, but it takes practice.

- You are negotiating with a very small company. They claim to have resources far and above those you know they can afford.
- A stakeholder is telling you about his problems with delivery. He won't meet your eye, often looking at the floor. He shifts a lot in his seat.
- A foreign stakeholder is very expansive, boastful even, about her position.
- The numbers don't add up in a stakeholder's presentation.

Feedback Here are some possible realities behind the observations. In the first example, the small company did have those resources, by calling on other companies. The shifty stakeholder was telling the truth, but was worried because he hadn't been involved in a high level negotiation before. The boastful stakeholder was mostly responding to a cultural norm that is different to yours. She was also trying to cover up a weakness in her pitch. In the final example, there was a simple error, no attempt at deceit, but it does give you a position of superiority that may help in negotiation.

If you have suspicions, tread cautiously and ask yourself 'why?' – you might have misread the situation. Encourage the stakeholders to give more information. Make it easy for them to back out – defensive pride can devastate a negotiation. If you haven't got anywhere, try being upfront. Ask what's wrong. Be honest about your concerns. And if there's still no response, make it clear the lengths you will go to in order to make sure everything is OK.

Outcome This short exercise mostly concerns raising awareness of the difficulties of reading a lie or misrepresentation. If you can take charge when the truth is in doubt, you are more likely to get a favourable outcome.

Variations None.

Strategic	✪
Intuitive	✪✪✪✪
Process	✪
Fun	✪✪

5.7 | *Upping the game*

Preparation None.
Running time 10 minutes.
Resources None.
Timing Once.

Sometimes it seems as if you are completely outgunned. Try out this exercise before reading the feedback section. You are in a sales negotiation. The buyer is not impressed. He tells you that your bid is too expensive, your delivery dates unacceptable and your product is simply not of high enough quality. It seems as if you are totally shot out of the water. What do you do?

Feedback   The title of the exercise is a bit of a giveaway. When things seem to be going badly wrong with your negotiation, you can sometimes save the day by changing the level at which the negotiation operates. Open up a longer-term picture. Show how the competition might have the lead right now (often this can imply a criticism, for instance, because their product is out of date, hence quicker to manufacture), but in the longer term you have all the cards. Pull in other products and services – give a system view instead of a single-product view. (IBM did a wonderful job in the 1980s of tying in corporate clients by negotiating on the basis of a stunning architecture that spanned mainframes to PCs. Obviously no one else could do this. In fact, the full architecture never materialized, but the system view won an awful lot of negotiations before this became obvious.) Emphasize your people benefits, too. But don't make all this wishy-washy; make sure you have real illustrations involving real situations. If you are forced into this sort of 'soft benefit' arguing, try to emphasize your ethical stance. Soft arguments only hold up if you can show yourself to be open and straightforward. Don't put the opposition down, but provide such great support that even if the deal goes a different way, the stakeholder will consider coming back to you in the future.

Outcome   When you are foundering on the current level, moving a negotiation up a level can change the playing field, bringing in considerations that weren't previously considered.

Variations   None.

Strategic   ✪
Intuitive   ✪✪✪
Process   ✪✪✪
Fun   ✪✪

5.8 | *Paper mountains*

Preparation None.
Running time Five minutes.
Resources Incoming documents.
Timing Daily.

Getting background information is appropriate for good negotiation, but too much paper can result in overload. This time-management exercise can help to deal with the paper input that accompanies every negotiation. Paper needs chunking. Don't read each item as it hits your desk, but pull them together at sensible intervals – perhaps once or twice a day – to fit your working pattern. Even if you are in the middle of a heavy negotiation, it's probably worth taking time off to do this – otherwise you might miss something essential.

Take a couple of minutes over a first pass. Sort paper into three types. Junk, items requiring action and items requiring reading. Practise making this decision within a few seconds. Check the heading and the first paragraph – you ought to have made a decision by then. Commercial junk is probably best trashed, but reports and other internal documents are different. Write in large, red letters at the top (even better, get a stamp – it's very satisfying) 'returned unread' and send it back. This is particularly valuable in a culture where you may be criticized for not taking action – here you have taken a very clear action.

Feedback You may get people contacting you who assume you have read a document. You can try: honesty ('It didn't look relevant, so I didn't read it', or 'I don't know'), distraction ('Remind me what it was about'), or deception ('Yes?'). Each is valid – see which suits you best.

Outcome The principle aim is to avoid wasting time, but there are secondary benefits. For instance, sending back items marked 'unread' may make the sender consider stopping production of the offending article. To the negotiator, time is crucial. By taking this approach, you can make sure that all input gets dealt with on the same day, so minimizing the chances of a document that is crucial to the negotiation slipping through your fingers.

Variations Apply a similar regime to e-mails – chunk them up for dealing with in handfuls several times a day.

Strategic	✪✪✪
Intuitive	✪
Process	✪✪✪✪
Fun	✪✪✪

5.9 | *Talking yourself down*

Preparation None.
Running time Two minutes.
Resources None.
Timing Once.

You can be one of your own worst enemies in a selling negotiation. Unless you are as hard as nails and don't give a damn about anyone else, the chances are you don't like to upset people – in fact, you quite like to please them. So before they've even got a chance to speak you can end up talking yourself down.

For example, you are asked 'What's your hourly rate?' (or unit price, or whatever), and you say '£100'. All of a sudden that sounds a trifle excessive. After all, you are dealing with a small company, or you've heard they are in financial difficulties, or the negotiator has a nice face. So you quickly add, 'But of course, it's negotiable'. Why not just stab yourself in the back straight away?

In fact, you can attack yourself without even adding the rider. If you answer 'Around the £100 mark', or something similar, you are actively inviting the other stakeholders to lower your price for you. Even the number 100 sounds like a negotiating stance; £99 or £101 might be better.

Feedback The other stakeholders are going to make it their goal to chip away at your price anyway without you helping them out. Now that you are aware of this danger, make sure that you are very clear about your price upfront – and very happy that it is a sensible price to ask. Now, get it fixed in your mind that this is the price that you are asking, however pathetic the other negotiators look. And tell them as if you were doing them a favour, not apologetically. Why should you apologize about your price if it's fair?

Outcome This is a painless exercise that will increase your chances of getting a reasonable price in an instant. Don't give way to temptation.

Variations None.

Strategic	✪
Intuitive	✪✪✪✪
Process	✪
Fun	✪✪

5.10 | **Waiting room**

Preparation None.
Running time Five minutes.
Resources Bag or briefcase.
Timing Regularly.

Most of us spend too long waiting before, during and after negotiations. You turn up three minutes early and wait for 20 minutes before everyone else is ready to start. So you read a business magazine or chat. Time is slipping away. It is time wasting, and it's stressful.

Some time management experts suggest leaving a message to say you will be in your office getting some work done, and would like a call when the other stakeholders are present. Unfortunately, this is impractical off-site and dangerous on-site. Either you end up playing call-me tag, waiting for everyone to finish a task, or you seriously disrupt the negotiations. Instead, carry a package of portable tasks. Things you can get on with while you wait. It could be your mail, or writing a memo – anything you can do using only the contents of your bag.

Feedback   You may be regarded as a little strange if others are waiting in the same place. If they don't have tasks to get on with, they might expect you to contribute to their chat. There isn't a right or wrong answer, it depends on who they are and the relevance of the conversation. It may end up being a preliminary to the negotiation proper – but it may be a complete waste of time.

Outcome   Making use of such unplanned snippets of time is a great way of chipping away at background activities. You are, in effect, generating time from nowhere, relieving stress and making sure you are in the best state to start negotiating when the others are ready.

Variations   A laptop or palmtop computer makes an ideal mobile task kit. If you are waiting for someone else to arrive, undertake a task that can be stopped at a moment's notice. It doesn't get things off to a good start if the others have to watch you finish something off for 10 minutes.

Strategic	✪
Intuitive	✪
Process	✪✪✪
Fun	✪✪

5.11 | **Go casual**

Preparation Negotiation organized.
Running time Variable.
Resources None.
Timing Once.

Formal negotiations eat up time and often get bogged down. Yet face-to-face meetings are the best way to achieve a result. A high proportion of important decisions come out of informal meetings; not a group sat around a board table in a stuffy office, but casual get-togethers around the coffee machine, or chance meetings in the corridor. The same could work for a negotiation.

Here's a challenge then. Take a minor negotiation you are due to have in the next couple of weeks and move it to a casual location. It might be a coffee bar or a park – I've had meetings in car parks, but ideally it should be somewhere you can get comfortable, but not have the formal, stuffy surroundings of a meeting room. It should be a session that doesn't require lots of technical support like electronic whiteboards or computers. See how it feels. In most cases, you will have a much better, more productive negotiation.

Feedback Sessions of this sort tend to be shorter than a traditional negotiation, yet don't have the feeling of time pressure that can result in bad decisions. They get through more, yet improve interpersonal relations – all to the good for both your business and personal goals. And they make meetings more enjoyable. Surely, anything that can make meetings more enjoyable is worthwhile.

Outcome This isn't a technique you will use for every negotiation, but it is worth bringing out in certain cases. For sessions that tend to get bogged down and overrun, for negotiations where atmosphere is important, this approach is ideal.

Variations The possible locations can be very varied. To keep it really short, have the session standing up – it sounds bizarre, but it is possible. It might mean taking down actions on a pocket recorder and transcribing them later, but it could be worth it if you have a time-keeping problem.

Strategic ✪
Intuitive ✪✪✪
Process ✪✪✪✪
Fun ✪✪✪

5.12 | *Using emotion*

Preparation None.
Running time Five minutes.
Resources Pen and paper.
Timing Once.

Emotions are an inevitable part of a negotiation. It might seem logical to try to remove emotion and make a negotiation clinical, but in fact emotions can work to your benefit. Spend five minutes considering how you might employ the following emotions in a negotiation. Don't go on to the feedback section until you have done this.

- Anger.
- Warmth.
- Excitement.
- Gut feel.

Feedback Anger needs careful use. You should always be in control of it, rather than the other way round. Use anger as a short, sharp shock if you are being misused to express your distress. It should be switched off quickly as soon as there is a response, whether it's an apology or more anger. Positive emotions, like warmth and excitement, can be used a great deal more than they are. Warmth will help others to be comfortable with the deal. Excitement will stress your commitment and energy. When things are going well, put that excitement across, not in terms of 'I'm really stomping on you', but 'We're getting along excellently'. Gut feel is a special case. It's very important – your reaction to what is happening is just as important as the numbers, but make sure that your gut feel is applied correctly. Gut feel is great on concepts and directions, but often lousy on numbers. Almost everyone's gut feel can be misled by statistics, and even as simple a concept as percentages can confuse – be wary of small percentages of large numbers, as they seem insignificant, but can, of course, be just as significant as large percentages of small numbers. Go with your gut feel, but do so after conscious and cool assessment.

Outcome Using emotion correctly can tip the balance your way in a negotiation that is logically straightforward. We are emotional beings, so any attempt to ignore emotion will play into the hands of those who use it.

Variations None.

Strategic	✪✪✪
Intuitive	✪✪✪✪
Process	✪
Fun	✪✪✪

5.13 | *Competitive pressure*

Preparation None.
Running time Five minutes.
Resources Pen and paper.
Timing Once.

Imagine that you are in a position of trying to sell a single product to a number of possible buyers. You are outnumbered and the buyers are much more significant players than you are. Jot down ways that you can, judo style, use the power of the other buyers to bring pressure on a negotiation.

Feedback The most popular approach is the combination of a fictional bid and time pressure. Approach stakeholder A and say that if they are going do anything they had better do it quickly as another stakeholder has already made an offer. This time pressure makes the stakeholder more likely to act on incomplete information (the inverse of *Slowing the pace*, 5.48). You may even find it can start a stampede amongst competitive stakeholders. Time pressure isn't always necessary, though. An alternative is to use the advantages to you of one potential customer to sell to others. Saying what a great opportunity there is to work with company A may significantly weaken companies B and C's positions.

What you are trying to do in such circumstances is to transform the situation from you selling to the buyers, to the buyers selling to you, competing to buy your products and services. This can be achieved, but it is a high-risk tactic and is best applied when you are in a negotiation that you are relatively unlikely to succeed in, but which would be very high value.

Outcome By bringing external power to bear you are increasing your strength in the negotiation. Look for these external advantages when the other stakeholder has competitors.

Variations You might not often be involved in this style of negotiation, but the influence of pressure from other stakeholders may apply in many negotiations.

Strategic ✪
Intuitive ✪✪✪
Process ✪✪
Fun ✪✪✪

5.14 | *Breathing is good for you*

Preparation None.
Running time Two minutes.
Resources None.
Timing Regularly.

This exercise, developed from one in *Instant Stress Management* (see page 127), is a great one for dealing with pressure on the spot in a negotiation. It's a self-evident truth that breathing is a good thing – but there's breathing and there's breathing. Firstly, as all singers know, there are two types of breathing – with the chest muscles and with the diaphragm. The latter is more controlled and gives you a much deeper breath, yet it tends to be underused, particularly by those under stress.

When you've a couple of minutes to spare on your own, try to feel that diaphragmatic breathing. Stand up straight, but not tense. Take a deep breath and hold it for a second. Your chest will rise. Now try to keep your chest in the 'up position' while breathing in and out. You should feel a tensing and relaxing around the stomach area. Rest a hand gently on your stomach to feel it in action.

Once you've got the feel for diaphragmatic breathing you can use it anywhere – for instance, in a negotiation. Close your eyes if you can do so without appearing rude. Begin to breathe regularly: count up to five (in your head!) as you breathe in through your nose. Hold it for a second, then breathe out through your mouth, again counting to five. Don't consciously force your rib cage to stay up now, but concentrate on movement of the diaphragm. Your stomach should gently rise as you breathe in and fall as you breathe out.

Feedback A breathing exercise like this can be performed pretty well anywhere, making it ideal for in-negotiation relief.

Outcome A regular session of breathing properly will provide the foundation for many other stress management techniques. It is simple and very effective in dealing with stress, which can be a major issue in negotiation.

Variations Don't miss out on this one – it involves little effort and it is very valuable.

Strategic	✪✪✪✪
Intuitive	✪✪✪
Process	✪✪✪✪
Fun	✪✪✪

5.15 | *The power of print*

Preparation None.
Running time 10 minutes.
Resources Books, brochures, company documents, Web access.
Timing Once.

There is something very special about the printed word. The more you can back up your case in a negotiation with print, the better chance you have of movement in your direction. This doesn't seem entirely logical, but it works. If you appear to be plucking figures out of the air, the other stakeholders will be suspicious. If, however, you have documentation to support those figures – even if it is documentation you have written (for example, a price list) – the numbers will have more credibility. The same goes for anything, from endorsements for your products and services to criticism of a competitor.

Bear in mind that the printed word has a hierarchy of values. A book, newspaper or magazine comes highest (except in academic circles, where a paper will top even these). After this comes your own printed information, and finally typed information. Net-based information, while technically no more substantial than your own typed print, tends to come more on a par with your professionally printed material.

As an exercise, take 10 minutes to get together as much printed material as you can to support the effectiveness of one of your products or services. Bear in mind the hierarchy – try to get the best impact you can.

Feedback This strange belief in print does not weaken the need to establish a good personal relationship with the other stakeholders. Impassioned arguments and trust require verbal interaction. But print gives authority to any accompanying facts and figures. It acts as a buffer against attempts from the other stakeholders to get movement in your variables – you can hide behind the printed material.

Outcome Get used to assembling a printed support pack for your negotiation and you will have a better chance of fighting off pressure on key variables, by adding authority to the facts and figures you quote.

Variations None.

Strategic ✪✪✪
Intuitive ✪✪✪
Process ✪✪
Fun ✪✪

5.16 | *It's yours right now*

Preparation None.
Running time Two minutes.
Resources None.
Timing Once.

In some negotiations, theory and reality are widely separated. The other stakeholders know in their minds what the value of your offering is, but it's quite another thing to see it in the flesh. Whether you are buying or selling, trading or establishing facts, you can sometimes make a breakthrough in the negotiation by bringing reality to the table.

If you were selling something you could bring it to the table, or take the stakeholders to it and say 'Here it is. It's yours right now. Just…'. If you are buying, you can put cash or a cheque in front of them. Because it minimizes risk, the human urge to get something NOW if we can without waiting is very strong (just check out the subtitle of this book). If you can make that come true, especially with an actual physical presence on the spot, your chances of getting the negotiation to conclude successfully will be enhanced. Just spend a couple of minutes thinking through the practicalities of this approach for the sort of things you negotiate.

Feedback This harks back to one of the oldest techniques in the book – you see it in the movies all the time – slapping down the hard cash in front of someone's nose until they give way and accept it. It is, realistically, a very crude technique. But bearing in mind how much negotiation operates at the gut level, this isn't necessarily a bad thing. There are times when a figurative punch between the eyes can make all the difference.

Outcome By giving the stakeholders a view of the reality – and possibly the chance to walk away with it right now – you can maximize the chance of closing a deal.

Variations Even with an intangible like a job, you can employ a variant of this technique. If you are headhunting, for instance, don't talk in a distant agency office. Walk them through the job, expose them to the place and the people. Tell them 'This is all yours'.

Strategic	✪
Intuitive	✪✪✪✪
Process	✪
Fun	✪✪✪

5.17 | *Getting endorsements*

Preparation Target endorsers.
Running time 30 minutes.
Resources Mail and e-mail.
Timing Once.

All negotiation requires an element of trust. The more the other stakeholders trust you, the easier it is to get some movement. In most cases, the other parties to the negotiation don't know you very well. This is where endorsement can come in. If you can get a respected third party to endorse your input to the negotiation, it is liable to give more weight to your case.

Endorsements can be both about you as a person and about parts or all of your case in the negotiation. Who you get to provide the endorsement depends on a combination of willingness to take part and suitability. The important thing is that someone respected by one or more of the other stakeholders has come in on your side.

As an exercise, put together a list of people you have dealt with in the past six months who might be prepared to give you an endorsement. Why not go the extra mile, and actually ask for it, too?

Feedback Getting endorsements is something that feels harder than it actually is. It is easy to assume that you won't get endorsements, so you don't bother to try. And yet it often takes very little effort (beyond embarrassment) to get in touch with someone and ask for an endorsement. It's rare to get them if you don't ask.

While the obvious endorsers are other customers, if you are trying to sell something, you can consider a much wider range of people. Provided the subject of the negotiation is interesting, or your case is strong, it's surprising how often you can get perfect strangers to endorse your side. If those strangers happen to be famous or influential in the eyes of the other stakeholders you have got a real advantage.

Outcome Endorsements increase the value of your argument and make it more likely that the other stakeholders will move in your direction.

Variations Don't give way to embarrassment about contacting strangers if necessary – it will be worth it.

Strategic	✪
Intuitive	✪✪✪
Process	✪✪✪
Fun	✪

5.18 | *Exploring trust*

Preparation None.
Running time 15 minutes.
Resources Paper and pen.
Timing Once.

If you can establish a state of trust with the other stakeholders, you are much more likely to achieve a win–win outcome. This exercise helps you to explore the mechanics of trust. Spend five minutes thinking about the trusting relationships you have had. With family, friends, colleagues – and in negotiation. What made you trust the other people? How was the trust built up? Note some key factors.

Now take another five minutes to consider how those factors can be built into the negotiation process. For instance, one might be 'delivering on a promise'. What can you do during a negotiation to be seen to deliver on a promise? The delivery would have to take place before the negotiation was over to ensure that the stakeholder got the message. In a final five minutes, pull out the longer-term implications of trust. If you aren't just having a one-off negotiation, how can you use your key factors of trust to develop a trusting relationship over time? What should you avoid if you don't want to demolish trust?

Feedback Trust is probably the single most important success factor that is regularly absent from business. Parties in negotiations don't trust each other. Bosses don't trust workers. Workers don't trust bosses. Vendors don't trust customers (and vice versa). The need to establish trust is not out of a sense of moral values (although that isn't a bad thing) – it is demonstrably the only way to sustain a win–win relationship. If it seems strange that the archetype of trust I'm recommending for you to use is the trust within your existing relationships, it shouldn't be. Negotiation is a personal human interaction. Effective negotiation has to be based as much on your own characteristics as on any theory.

Outcome The exercise delivers a better understanding of how you can build trust. It's then up to you to put it into practice in your negotiations. If it's a big turn around, it may take a while before the other stakeholders believe you. Give it time.

Variations None; this is one you can't do without.

Strategic	✪✪✪✪
Intuitive	✪✪
Process	✪✪✪
Fun	✪✪✪

5.19 | *Basic option evaluation*

Preparation None.
Running time 15 minutes.
Resources Notepad, pen.
Timing Once.

Where you have a number of options to choose between, a simple option evaluation can make it much more practical to go for the right choice. Try out this exercise on a real life evaluation, like choosing a new car.

List the options on a piece of paper. If there are more than three or four, try to eliminate some immediately as totally unacceptable.

Now list the criteria by which you will decide between options. What will you use to distinguish them? Again, keep to a handful of the most important criteria.

Finally, score each option against each criterion. Either use a 1–10 scale or a High/Medium/Low scale. Combine the results.

This should give you a ranking of the options according to these logical criteria. However, it shouldn't be used as a fixed decision, but rather as a guide to put alongside your intuition. If your gut feel differs from the logical assessment, try to see why. Are there criteria you are ignoring? Are some much more important than others?

Feedback Options can arise at several stages in a negotiation. You could be choosing between different bids, between different suppliers and products, between different combinations of variables. The only requirement is that you have a known set of options to choose between. This process helps you to understand your decision better and to come to a more effective choice.

Outcome By taking a systematic approach you can ensure that you have considered all the options, and that you are picking one with a conscious awareness of the criteria by which you will make the choice – the outcome is a more rational, thought-through decision.

Variations If you are finding wide variation between criteria, try *Sophisticated option evaluation*, 5.20.

Strategic ✪
Intuitive ✪
Process ✪✪✪✪
Fun ✪✪

5.20 Sophisticated option evaluation

Preparation None.
Running time 20 minutes.
Resources Notepad, pen.
Timing Once.

Sometimes, criteria aren't enough to decide between options. You need to be able to give different weightings to say that, for example, price is twice as important as delivery times. The process used is much the same as in *Basic option evaluation*, 5.19, but will take a little longer. As before, use the selection of a new car, or something similar, for the exercise.

List the options on a piece of paper. Even more so than with a basic evaluation, it is important you restrict the list to perhaps three or four. Then list the criteria by which you will decide between options. What will you use to distinguish them? Again, keep to a handful of the most important criteria. Before going any further weigh the criteria. Give one criterion the value of 1 and give each other a value that reflects its relative importance compared with that key criterion – for example, if it's half as important, give it a value 0.5. If it's twice as important, make it 2.

Finally, score each option against each criterion using a 1–10 scale. When you have, multiply each score by the criterion weightings before adding up the results.

This should give you a ranking of the options according to these logical criteria. However, it should only be a guide to put alongside intuition. If your gut feel differs from the logical assessment, try to see why. Are there criteria you are ignoring?

Feedback Options arise at several stages in a negotiation. You could be choosing between bids, between different suppliers and products, between different combinations of variables. Adding weighting to the process makes the evaluation more finely tuned.

Outcome By taking a systematic approach you can ensure that you have considered all the options, and that you are picking one with a conscious awareness of the criteria by which you will make the choice – the outcome is a more rational, thought-through decision.

Variations If the numbers are getting a bit of a strain, you may find it helpful to use a spreadsheet instead of paper.

Strategic ✪
Intuitive ✪
Process ✪✪✪✪
Fun ✪✪

5.21 | *Options with guts*

Preparation *Sophisticated option evaluation*, 5.20
Running time 15 minutes.
Resources Notepad, pen.
Timing Once.

Logic can only take you so far – but many successful business decisions are based on gut feel. Does that mean you can ignore the concept of option evaluation? Not at all – but you need to flex the result. As a starting point, you will need the output of the *Sophisticated option evaluation* exercise. Look at the outcomes. Re-rank the options according to your feeling. Don't worry about the detail and the criteria, how would you rank them yourself? If there is a difference between your gut-feel ranking and the mechanical one, get an idea of what it would take to move from the 'official' evaluation to yours. Play around with some of the criteria to see if you could make your gut-feel ranking come true by altering the scores or weights. For instance, you might be able to increase an option's ranking by decreasing the importance of price and increasing the importance of appearance (or whatever criteria you used). If there isn't a difference, you are a very logical person. Don't give up on the exercise, though. Play around with the scores and weights to see how sensitive the outcome is to changes.

Feedback Getting a feel for the ease with which you can change a decision is extremely valuable in coming to the right outcome. Performing this sort of sensitivity analysis can really help to get a handle on what you are doing in preferring a particular option. Unfortunately, the numbers quickly get messy, especially when there are several variables. There are a number of computer software packages on the market to assist with decision analysis (a spreadsheet alone isn't ideal, although it's better than nothing). Check the Creativity Unleashed software site at **www.cul.co.uk/software**.

Outcome As we've seen, options arise when choosing between different bids, between different suppliers and products, between different combinations of variables, and so on. If you can understand the logical choice, and how much you have to contort it to match your gut-feel outcome, you are in the best position possible.

Variations None.

Strategic   ✪
Intuitive   ✪✪✪
Process   ✪✪✪✪
Fun   ✪✪

5.22 | *Reading upside down (no, really!)*

Preparation None.
Running time Five minutes.
Resources None.
Timing Several times.

There's something faintly embarrassing about this one, but the fact is that the better your information is, the better your negotiating stance. It is not uncommon to come across information on pieces of paper that happen to be facing away from you on a desk. Being able to read these with the text upside down can be very valuable.

All it takes is a little practice. Get a wide range of documents and put them upside down on a table. Try to read each as quickly as possible. Don't bend over, or peer specifically at the document. You will find you need quite a different style to normal reading, something closer to the reading of a young child, where you read each word instead of chunks of text at a time. Persevere and you will find that your speed notches up. Try both handwritten and printed text.

Feedback   This seems rather sneaky. But you aren't rifling through other people's drawers, you are just taking in information that has been left openly available for perusal. The fact that it's upside down is neither here nor there.

I ought to clarify also that, when I say the documents to be read should be upside down on a table, I don't mean face down. There are limits to what even this book can achieve.

Outcome   If reading upside down becomes a natural skill, you will increase your chances of having the right information to make the negotiation go your way.

Variations   Take the opportunity to practise every time you see an upside-down document. Apart from giving you exercise, it may help with a negotiation. Don't ignore papers just because they're the right way up, though. The point is to be generally observant.

Strategic	✪✪
Intuitive	✪
Process	✪✪✪
Fun	✪✪✪✪

5.23 | *Starting prices*

Preparation None.
Running time 10 minutes.
Resources None.
Timing Once.

Selling requires a starting price. Setting it makes most inexperienced negotiators uncomfortable. Try making a decision on each of these right now.

- You are a selling a house that has unusual construction. The agent recommends starting it at 20 per cent under the typical market price. What would you do?
- You have written an excellent business book, but it's quite short. Books of this length typically sell for £9.99, but the publisher wants to sell it at £16.99 to focus on the senior management market. How would you react?
- Your company is bidding to provide a regular service for another company. Your first stab at a price is £150,000, but your accountant finds out that most of the competition are coming in around £100,000. What would you do?

Note down what you would do, including a couple of reasons in each case.

Feedback   In the first case, marking the house down says there is something wrong with it. I'd suggest starting at 20 per cent above market price for a unique opportunity. With the book, I'd suggest £79.99 with an expensive binding and a sales pitch emphasizing value and executive appeal. In the third case, I would bid £110,000, emphasizing there was no room for movement as the bid should have been £150,000, reflecting our quality, but we really value working with them.

Outcome   Being able to set a bold but appropriate starting price is a great asset. Note that appropriate doesn't mean sustainable, just worthy of discussion.

Variations   Experiment with real but safe negotiations.
    Beef up the competition. It's a risky strategy because the other stakeholders may say, 'OK, go with them', but some very effective negotiations have been concluded because it looked like a fictional competitor would get the business. This works best if there really is competition, but the competitor doesn't quite make the grade.

Strategic	✪✪✪
Intuitive	✪✪✪
Process	✪✪✪✪
Fun	✪✪✪

5.24 | *Playing poker*

Preparation None.
Running time Five minutes.
Resources Pen and paper.
Timing Once.

There's a paradox that faces every negotiator at some time or other. You can't afford to lie, because it endangers trust, and it's unethical – but you can't afford to tell the truth either, because it will destroy any chance you have of winning through.

Spend a few minutes coming up with different ways that you can lie without really lying – indulging in a poker-hand bluff.

Feedback   In many negotiations you may not need this technique, but it would be ridiculous to suggest that it hasn't been very valuable to many negotiators over the years. It needs to be used with care, and not overplayed. There are a number of potential components:

- Saying you will do something that you wouldn't really. Probably. The classic large-scale example of this is deterrent-based negotiations on the world stage.
- Claiming that you can deliver something that you don't have the capability to deliver. But you could find a way. For instance, a small company might go for a large contract, saying it has the resources to meet it. In fact it will bring in third-party contractors, but will oversee the contract and make sure that delivery occurs.
- Beefing up the competition. It's a risky strategy, because the other stakeholders may say 'OK, go with them', but some very effective negotiations have been concluded because it looked like a fictional competitor would get the business. This works best if there really is competition, but the competitor doesn't quite make the grade.
- Invoking fictional deadlines and pressures. It is quite often helpful to put a little time pressure on a negotiation. If there isn't a real cause, invent one.

Outcome   This isn't the most likeable tactic, but can be effective in pushing a negotiation into completion. To be handled with care.

Variations   None.

Strategic	✪
Intuitive	✪✪✪✪
Process	✪
Fun	✪✪✪

5.25 | *Another lever*

Preparation *The agreement space*, 5.4.
Running time 10 minutes.
Resources None.
Timing Once.

There is always another lever to pull. You will see this coming out in various techniques throughout this book, but it is worth emphasizing as a general concept because it is so important. Your ability to negotiate depends on making movements in the various variables under your control. In a sales negotiation, for instance, such variables will generally include price, quantities, delivery costs, timing and so forth.

When undertaking a negotiation, you should always be using these variables to get concessions out of the other stakeholders. The good news is that however many variables you think there are, there can always be more.

Before any negotiation, take 10 minutes to think about the variables. Set yourself the task of adding two more (although it may be that you can find many). Get them lined up, considering their potential impact on the stakeholders and their impact on you. Don't let the other negotiators win the lever war. As an exercise, take the set of variables you used in *The agreement space*, 5.4, and add two more.

Feedback Just as a good card player keeps his or her cards well hidden, you don't want all your levers exposed upfront. Keep a few winners back to pull out in case the other stakeholders come up with something difficult to handle. Remember to think outside the individual product to anything your company and the stakeholder companies are (or could be) involved in.

Outcome The ability to add in another variable can both counter a surprise step from the other stakeholders and improve your own position in the negotiation.

Variations None.

Strategic ✪✪✪✪
Intuitive ✪✪
Process ✪✪✪✪
Fun ✪✪

5.26 | *Your USP*

Preparation None.
Running time 10 minutes.
Resources None.
Timing Once.

Whether or not you are literally selling in a negotiation, the act of negotiating will have an element of selling in it – selling your proposition, selling your side of the argument. In marketing, an important contributory factor is the USP – the unique selling proposition. Spend a few minutes thinking what your USP should be for a particular deal coming up. If you don't have one lined up, develop the USP for you as a person that you might use in getting a job.

A USP should be short, sharp and memorable, getting through to the key essence of the selling proposition in a single sentence. It might be as broad as 'Never knowingly undersold', or 'We try harder', or as specific as '20 per cent cheaper than any competitor', or 'The only all-night chemist that delivers'.

Feedback You may not necessarily come out with your USP in a negotiation (although if it's a good one, you ought to – and to hammer it home however you can). Even if you don't, it's valuable to have it in mind as a focus for your argument of why things should go your way.

If your negotiation is primarily about finding an acceptable outcome – for instance union negotiations with a company – don't make the assumption that this isn't for you. Like it or not, you are still selling your position, your point of view. Even if the whole concept of selling is one that sits uncomfortably, you can benefit from a USP for a negotiation.

Outcome As a condensation of the unique value of the proposition, the USP has proved a fundamental marketing tool – it can also benefit anyone involved in a negotiation.

Variations None.

Strategic	✪✪✪✪
Intuitive	✪✪✪
Process	✪✪✪✪
Fun	✪✪

5.27 | ***Setting targets***

Preparation *The agreement space*, 5.4.
Running time 30 minutes.
Resources None.
Timing Once.

When you are sitting in a negotiation and pressure is coming from all directions, it is not the time to be indulging in higher mathematics. It's then that any preparation you can put in pays off. This exercise focuses on two prime targets – trade-offs and final positions.

Using the same example as in *The agreement space*, 5.4, put together a list of variables. For each draw up a table showing the best, worst and fair outcome. The best outcome is the value that you could reach if everything went your way, being realistic. The worst is the value beyond which you simply couldn't go because it would make the whole negotiation non-viable. The fair value is one that you would be comfortable with, being neither outstanding nor disastrous. On the same sheet of paper, if possible, draw up some potential trade-offs. Consider the variables in combination. If the other stakeholders gave way on one variable, what would you give in return? You will find it useful to undertake *The agreement space*, 5.4, before doing this exercise, as it will make it clearer what an effective trade-off would be.

Feedback   As an exercise, try this out for a fictional negotiation (or even better, a historical negotiation that you have information about). Note *Another lever*, 5.25, when undertaking this exercise. Once you have got your targets together, take a few minutes to look for other variables that you could bring into the equation.

Outcome   A positions and trade-offs document is one of the most important you can take into a negotiation. If you have a superb memory, you would be best memorizing it. If you can't manage this, make sure it is in a form that you can read easily – but the other stakeholders can't (see *Reading upside down*, 5.22).

Variations   Use your targets when practising. Come up (or even better get someone else to come up) with a series of random movements of variables. See how you would react, given your targets.

Strategic	✪✪✪✪
Intuitive	✪✪
Process	✪✪✪✪
Fun	✪✪

5.28 | *Play that back*

Preparation None.
Running time Five minutes.
Resources A stooge.
Timing Several times.

Unless you can really take in what the other stakeholders are saying, you are unlikely to get the best out of a deal. In *Hearing what they really say*, 5.5, we focus on ensuring that you give real attention to listening, but that alone is not enough. Language isn't always great at communicating what we really mean. If you are really to listen, you also need to make sure that what you heard is what the other stakeholder thought he or she said.

Get a friend or colleague to talk to you about something they feel passionately about, but you know very little about. Every minute or two, feed back to them what you think they said. Try this several times over a few weeks.

Feedback Sounding back what you think you have heard is a primary tool of the communicator. Without it you can never be sure that there hasn't been a breakdown of understanding, leading to all the confusion possible in a game of Chinese Whispers. Make sure you use different words, don't just echo exactly what you heard (a parrot can do this). It's possible for this feeding-back process to seem threatening, as if it is a criticism of what has been said. If you feel that the other stakeholder is getting fed up with it, say something like 'I'm sorry, I'm just not with it today. Can I just make sure I've got this right. You want to…'. This way, the blame for the implied misunderstanding is on you, not on the other person.

Outcome Listening well is the hardest part of communicating. Unless you listen well your communications will suffer, and so will your negotiation. Testing what you heard increases your chances of getting it right.

Variations Like most communication skills, this benefits from repeated practice. Look for other opportunities to play back conversations and check understanding.

Strategic	✪✪
Intuitive	✪✪✪
Process	✪
Fun	✪✪

5.29 | **Subverting a meeting**

Preparation None.
Running time Five minutes.
Resources Minutes of a meeting.
Timing Once.

Take the minutes of a meeting you have attended. Look at each item in the minutes. If it had not been written down, what scope is there for misunderstanding what was said and what was agreed? Are there clear action points? If there are, what would happen if they weren't there? If there aren't, what should have been minuted to make sure that actions took place?

Feedback Although a meeting isn't always an explicit negotiation, it always contains elements of negotiation and often will turn into a full-scale example. However, it doesn't really matter for the purpose of the exercise; the issue here is the importance of putting things in writing to make things clear after the event. It is essential that someone notes down exactly what happened in the negotiation and gets the agreement of those involved. Ideally, this should be you – not because you would misrepresent the truth, though you could certainly make sure it is not shaded against you. Such notes needn't be lengthy. They should be limited to outcomes and actions (unless some aspect of the process has to be captured to make it clear how the outcome was reached).

This exercise is related to *The power of print*, 5.15, but rather than being about using written material before the event, this is about using written material afterwards. Once again, print will lend authority to your argument, but this time in terms of what was said.

Outcome Getting into the habit of making notes in a negotiation and circulating them to those involved is a valuable way to ensure that the outcome is carried through. A good approach is to e-mail notes to those involved within hours of completing the session, minimizing the opportunity for misunderstanding to creep in.

Variations None.

Strategic ✪✪
Intuitive ✪
Process ✪✪
Fun ✪✪

5.30 | **Knowing the opposition**

Preparation None.
Running time 10 minutes.
Resources Pen and paper.
Timing Once.

When you are undertaking a selling negotiation you will often be compared with your competitors. This exercise is only for those who have competitors – but realistically, that's most of us.

Spend two minutes noting down who your main competitors are (if necessary limit this to the competitors involved in a recent negotiation). Then for each competitor, list their main products and services. Note also how your products and services are better than theirs, and how their products and services are better than yours.

Feedback You may well find that you know a lot more about your products' benefits than you do about those of your competitors. PR people and salesmen quite often use 'silver bullets', documents that list all the advantages their products have over the competition. However, realistically, there will be some ways that the competitors' products are better – and if you don't know what they are, you will appear ignorant in negotiation or, even worse, it may seem as if you are trying to mislead the other stakeholders, destroying any trust you may have built up. Of course you don't need to brag about your shortcomings, but you shouldn't try to conceal them either. Instead, make them a feature. Point out how these are areas where it doesn't do to be at the leading edge, or emphasize how your new developments won't take you a little way ahead, as the competitors are, but leap over this generation entirely.

If you found that you didn't know a lot about your competitors' products and services, book time in your diary to find out now.

Outcome Knowing your competitors' products and their strengths will only help you in your negotiation. Think of a military campaign – intelligence is essential.

Variations None.

Strategic ✪✪✪✪
Intuitive ✪
Process ✪✪✪✪
Fun ✪✪

5.31 | *Broken CD*

Preparation Invent scenario.
Running time Five minutes.
Resources A stooge.
Timing Once.

Imagine a situation in which you have a point to put across in a negotiation that you simply have to succeed with. Persuade a colleague to act as a stooge in trying out this scenario. They are to counter your requirement. For example, you could be saying you need an order of at least a hundred items, or that you can't work at weekends. Think of at least half a dozen different ways of asking to have the same point accepted. They should be as different as possible without actually varying the outcome. Try different phrasing. Probe the other person for aspects of the point that they don't understand or have trouble with.

Feedback Sometimes when you are making a perfectly reasonable point you will be resisted. This exercise gives some practice in dealing with such a possibility by being assertive. Make sure that you keep your repeated requests low key and friendly. Nod, agree, say 'Yes, I see', to the other person's reasons for not coming up with the goods – then ask the same thing again in a different way. Like most negotiation techniques, this is best used face to face; it's too easy for the other person to just put the phone down. If you find it very difficult, practise some more – it becomes relatively easy and even enjoyable.

Outcome It is surprising how often this technique will whittle away resistance and get a result, and it can be less irritating than the pure broken record technique of repeating yourself without variation.

Variations If there is a genuine negotiation in which you can practise the technique, so much the better. You could also practise the technique when complaining about something or when you are trying to get information from a reluctant source.

Strategic   ✪
Intuitive   ✪✪✪
Process   ✪
Fun   ✪✪

5.32 | *Cut the aggro*

Preparation None.
Running time Five minutes.
Resources Pen and paper.
Timing Once.

As you can see in *Using emotion*, 5.12, and *Delightful deals*, 5.40, emotion has a very positive part to play in negotiation. However, when emotion shades into aggression your chances of achieving win–win go out of the window.

You are in a negotiation. The other party has a sudden outburst of aggression, thumping the table and shouting. What do you do? Spend a couple of minutes thinking about real circumstances where this has happened. Jot down a few things that have helped. Try to associate these fixes (and the suggestions below) with aggression so they come back to you automatically. Because you are countering a natural fight/flight reaction you need to make the responses pop into your mind immediately when you encounter aggression. Revisit them on a regular basis.

Feedback Generally, it's useful to take a quick breather – attempting to do anything in the heat of the moment can fuel the anger. Then, a very useful technique is to divert the focus from people to the problem. However much the other stakeholders push in the direction of anger, stay calm and show how the obstacle to progress is the problem, not the people round the table.

As is often the case with emotional conflict, it can help to make the situation explicit. Explain that you don't like the atmosphere – that it isn't helping progress. Allow a few minutes time out. If necessary be firm and assertive (but not aggressive) about not taking this sort of abuse. Surprisingly often, the aggressive stakeholder doesn't realize that he or she is doing anything other than have an intense discussion. Making your feelings explicit can defuse the situation.

Outcome If you can substitute a calm response for the natural reaction to aggression, you are well on the way to recovering the negotiation.

Variations Try acting out this situation with a friend. Get him or her to become angry with you. It's hard not to feel the emotional response even in this artificial circumstance. Then practise your response.

Strategic ✪
Intuitive ✪✪✪✪
Process ✪
Fun ✪✪

5.33 | **Which way?**

Preparation None.
Running time Five minutes.
Resources Diary, pen and paper.
Timing Once.

This exercise won't necessarily seem to have much to do with negotiation – bear with it, though. Get out your diary and work back to the last meeting you attended. Spend a few minutes jotting down just what the goals were of this meeting or series of meetings. What was the overall direction of the meeting? What short-term and long-term outcomes were intended? Now think about the meeting itself. Were these goals obvious throughout the meeting? Was there a clear focus on them?

Feedback   Although the exercise itself isn't specifically about negotiations, it is concerned with a major contributory factor to bad negotiation – lack of clear goals. Unless you go into a negotiation with a very clear picture of just what you are trying to attain – and in a large negotiation this may involve quite a complex mix of shorter and longer-term goals – you have little chance of success. It is essential before you start a negotiation that you clarify the goals.

I used meetings for the exercise as they often manage to drift from their original goals. Getting a clear focus and sticking to it wouldn't hurt your meetings either. Try checking on this next time you are in a meeting.

Outcome   Having a clear direction to aim for is essential in any negotiation.

Variations   Try bouncing your goals for a negotiation off several other people before beginning. You may find that you have only been considering a part of the requirement.

Strategic ✪✪✪✪
Intuitive ✪✪
Process ✪✪✪
Fun ✪✪

5.34 | **Terms of endearment**

Preparation None.
Running time Five minutes.
Resources Pen and paper.
Timing Once.

A simple exercise, but a useful reminder. Imagine two scenarios: (a) you are selling services costing £20,000; (b) you are buying the same services. For both, list as many different ways as you can to use terms of payment to get movement in your direction.

Feedback For the seller, a classic route is to offer finance, where you won't get the money upfront, but will make a profit on the process. You can also look to tie the purchaser in by terms of payment, offering lower costs if they agree to take a number of repeat orders, or using an automated payment method like direct debit that enables you to manage the payment process. You can give the buyer incentives to pay upfront. Sometimes, just asking for payment on the spot can be enough – or you can offer low-cost options like cheaper support in exchange for prompt payment. You can alternatively, of course, use any of the methods suggested below for a buyer in order to win over a customer without cutting into core costs. Book publishers have the buying technique sewn up – in a buyer's market, they hit authors several different ways (sorry, Kogan Page!). The initial advance payment is split into several instalments, typically on signing the contract, receiving the manuscript and publishing the book. The actual royalty payments are only made once or twice a year, meaning that the money is in the publishers' hands for a good length of time, decreasing the value of the payment. Of course, the publishers will argue there are lots of good reasons for this – but that's what good negotiating is all about. When you are buying, learn from the publisher. Try to split the payment, and push the payment date out. Tie it to some event that makes it almost reasonable. You could also ask for interest-free credit. These are just some ideas – you may have had better ones. The important thing is to get into the habit of thinking about terms. These examples have mostly been about price – remember, too, that you can modify terms in all different directions. See, for example, 5.39.

Outcome It's easy to be blinded by price. Remember that appropriate terms of payment can change the entire meaning of price to your company. Use them creatively.

Variations None.

Strategic	❂❂❂
Intuitive	❂❂❂
Process	❂❂❂❂
Fun	❂❂

5.35 | *Future visions*

Preparation Read up on a negotiation.
Running time Five minutes.
Resources Pen and paper.
Timing Once.

Find a negotiation that is just about to start or is under way. It could involve your company, or just be a negotiation that is in the news. Read up as much you can on the negotiation (this isn't part of the five minutes).

Now take a pen and paper and try to put down a word picture of the ideal outcome from your viewpoint. If you are any good at drawing, you might like to include actual pictures, too. Capture as much as you can in this vision of the way things could be as a result of the negotiation.

Feedback All negotiations are about the future, something that we can't see. Because the future is inevitably a fuzzy commodity, we all benefit from being handed concrete examples of what it is going to be like. This could be anything from a description, through an artist's impression to a full scale mock-up, depending on the resources you have and the type of negotiation that is under way.

It can be a huge benefit to your side of the discussion if you can realize a vision in this way, making the fuzzy possibilities of what might be into a clear future. The crudest version of this involves money – actually putting cash or a cheque into someone's hands (the technique described in *It's yours right now*, 5.16). 'Here you are, a cheque right now, if you accept the deal.' The physical presence of the cheque can seem much more real than the concept of payment. Similarly, anything that can be done to help the other stakeholders to visualize the outcome as you want it to be, and to make it seem more concrete, will help your chances of making it come true.

Outcome Human nature will ensure that the other stakeholders will prefer an outcome they can clearly visualize, or even touch. Help them to make it happen.

Variations None.

Strategic ✪
Intuitive ✪✪✪
Process ✪
Fun ✪✪✪

5.36 | *I'll be honest...*

Preparation None.
Running time Five minutes.
Resources None.
Timing Once.

You are in the midst of a negotiation to sell a single item. You have the following pieces of information. Which should you let the other stakeholder know?

1. You have been approached by two other potential buyers.
2. You have dealt with the stakeholder's competitors in the past.
3. You can't afford to drop the price much because of development costs.
4. Another potential buyer is ringing this afternoon.

Spend a couple of minutes jotting down what you would let them know in each case.

Feedback While we like to keep cards hidden, being more open will often get better results. In this example, I'd consider letting the other stakeholder know all four pieces of information. You may feel you need to protect your other potential buyers, but the knowledge of their existence may hurry things along. Just saying 'I have to be honest with you, I have two other companies interested', won't do a lot, because it sounds like a bluff, but with appropriate backup it can build towards openness and trust. The second item can be very powerful. Everyone is interested in competitors. While you won't give away trade secrets, the stakeholder will be interested to hear just how you got on with his or her competitor. For instance, when selling a book to a publisher, I usually take books I've written for other publishers. The publishers are genuinely interested in the way their competitors produce books and how they do business. Honesty on your reason for holding price can also reap dividends. If practical, show them a costing breakdown and why you have cut prices to the bone (of course, with appropriate mark-up – you have to survive). The more you can open up, the better the chances of winning the other stakeholder's confidence.

Outcome Opening up is a great way to encourage win–win, because you are both working on the same information base. It may encourage the other stakeholder to give more information too, and will certainly encourage trust.

Variations None.

Strategic	✪✪
Intuitive	✪✪✪
Process	✪
Fun	✪✪

5.37 | When you lose your temper

Preparation None.
Running time Five minutes.
Resources Pen and paper.
Timing Once.

Think back to the last time you *really* lost your temper. What were the first warning signs that you were getting angry? What did you say? How did you act? Were there things about the incident that you regretted later? Having thought through the incident, put together a checklist of actions you could take to counter uncontrolled anger.

Feedback Losing your temper in a negotiation wipes out any possibility of a win–win outcome until there has been a lot of work to undo the damage. It is much better if you don't lose your temper at all. Unfortunately, we are all human and many of us find that our tempers slip out of control before there's a chance to stop them, even if we are consciously trying to be restrained. A good action plan might be:

1. Get a five minute timeout. Get physically away from the others.
2. Do a quick breathing exercise (see *Breathing is good for you*, 5.14).
3. Think through what made you angry and try to put it into perspective, compared with the importance of the whole negotiation, or even the bigger perspectives of life.
4. Focus on the outcome, not the process.
5. Go back looking for ways to get round the problem, rather than just reacting to it.

But you need a plan that fits your temper and personality, so mix and match any ideas that seem to fit. Note, by the way, that controlling your temper does not mean you have to be soft with the other stakeholders all the time. It's like dealing with a child – you can tell them off and sound angry, but you shouldn't do it in a temper or you've lost control.

Outcome You will lose your temper occasionally, but this sort of preparation will give you the best chance of controlling it before negotiations are damaged.

Variations None.

Strategic ✪✪
Intuitive ✪
Process ✪✪✪
Fun ✪

5.38 | *Creative negotiation*

Preparation None.
Running time 15 minutes.
Resources None.
Timing Once.

Creativity is all about seeing a problem from a different viewpoint. Think of a negotiation you've been involved with in the past (or one that you have just known about, or heard about in the news) that became deadlocked.

Spend 10 minutes looking at ways that the negotiation could have been approached in different ways. If you know any creativity techniques, use them to come up with ideas. Or try:

*   thinking how a medieval monk would have got the negotiation moving;
*   thinking what would happen if one side, instead of saying 'This is what we want', said 'What do you think we should do to be satisfied?' to the other side;
*   asking why the stakeholders want the particular outcomes, then thinking of ways that they could be satisfied with totally different outcomes.

Feedback Creativity is something we all could have more of, and that helps in practically every negotiation. There's a list of books in Chapter 6 (see page 130) to help to build your creativity. The great thing about creativity is that it can often generate a win–win outcome where none was otherwise possible. Creativity doesn't have to be about releasing deadlock. It can also produce a better solution. Say you needed a widget to organize your office better. You could go out to vendors saying 'I want this type of widget, with this throughput and this performance rating, in green'. Or you could say 'I need to organize my office better, what do you recommend?' The second approach will get you a much wider span of options, bringing in the creativity of the different bidding teams. You then need a spot of creativity yourself to choose the option that will be most effective, rather than most predictable.

Outcome Bringing creativity into negotiation opens up the variables you can use, expands the range of options, gets round deadlocks and makes the whole process more interesting. It can't be bad.

Variations None.

Strategic	✪✪
Intuitive	✪✪✪
Process	✪✪✪✪
Fun	✪✪✪✪

5.39 | *Beautiful barter*

Preparation Prepare barter items.
Running time 10 minutes.
Resources Barter items.
Timing Once.

When selling, we often miss out on a real opportunity – barter. With barter, the goods or services you offer are worth cost price to you, but retail price to the other stakeholders: instant leverage. This means you can afford to be generous and still do well. Trade on retail price and each of you gets goods or services at cost. A wonderful win–win.

It may well be that you want to buy something from someone who doesn't need your goods or services. So what do you do? Find an intermediary. Someone who wants your output and has something desirable to the other party in your negotiation. Let's say that you were a holiday company and wanted to buy a fleet of vans. A garage is unlikely to want holidays. But your local radio station would love them as prizes. So barter your holidays for radio advertising, which can be offered to the garage, undercutting the radio station's rates. Again everyone benefits. The garage gets cheap advertising. The radio station gets a superb prize for 'free' slots, and you get your vans cheaply. You won't undertake barter in 10 minutes. The purpose of this exercise is to examine your products and services and determine what and how you can barter. Then next time you enter into a negotiation you will have a secret weapon.

Feedback A while ago, a major pharmaceutical company was negotiating with an airline to provide all its air travel. The pharmaceutical's purchasing director had recently flown with the airline and noticed that it used a competitor's products in its first-class soap bags. At a crucial point in the negotiation, he pointed this out. The airline changed its soap-bag supplier, and got the contract. No money changed hands to tip the balance – the movement was powered by barter.

Outcome Barter can change the face of a negotiation, bringing big percentages into play that weren't in the equation before. It's hard to understand why barter isn't used more.

Variations None.

Strategic ✪✪✪
Intuitive ✪✪✪✪
Process ✪✪✪✪
Fun ✪✪✪

5.40 | *Delightful deals*

Preparation None.
Running time Two minutes.
Resources None.
Timing Once.

It is easy to underestimate the emotional content of negotiation. Because numbers and facts are being bandied around we can forget that this is, in the end, a human interaction driven by very human responses. How stakeholders feel will influence the negotiation, whether you like it or not.

For this reason, there is a big benefit in encouraging a positive atmosphere during negotiation. Your best weapon is delight. Delight in your products or services. Delight in the pleasure of dealing with the other stakeholders. Delight in the win–win outcome.

Regularly, during the negotiation, remind yourself of all the good aspects that could come out of it. Smile at the other people. Force any negative thoughts away and think positively. You will be surprised at the results. As an exercise now, think through the last negotiation you were involved in. What could you have delighted in with a bit of effort? Don't let yourself say 'nothing' – come up with at least five things.

Feedback Like most positive emotions, delight is a lot harder to fake than a negative emotion. In fact, unless you've had lots of practice, the chances are that any attempt to fake delight will come across as false and smarmy. Instead, you will need to work on actually feeling delight. If you are selling, look for reasons to love your products or services. Whatever the negotiation, look for the good points in it. If you can get a good outcome, you and your company will benefit. That's something to look forward to, something to be positive about. Really try to enjoy the negotiation and the company of the other stakeholders. It might seem difficult to begin with, but it will come with practice.

Outcome Delight is a wonderful negotiating tool, as it is very delicate and yet powerful. Done right, it is almost irresistible. And you'll enjoy the process more yourself – not a bad side advantage.

Variations None.

Strategic	❂❂
Intuitive	❂❂❂❂
Process	❂❂❂
Fun	❂❂❂❂

5.41 | *Personality types*

Preparation None.
Running time Five minutes.
Resources None.
Timing Once.

People fall into a number of personality types. The exact number is open to debate, but the important thing for the negotiator is to be aware of how you tend to act, and how others do. Consider your answers to these questions:

- Do you prefer the big picture or getting down to detail?
- Do you prefer to work alone, or in a team?
- Are you motivated more by personal satisfaction or the praise of others?
- Do you find a regular progress check helpful or irritating?
- Do you draw up to-do lists for the week, or would you rather have broad objectives?
- Are you better at coming up with new ideas or developing and refining existing ones?
- What is more important, using the right process or succeeding?
- Are you more comfortable with an 80 per cent solution or striving for perfection?

Feedback You answered these questions in a particular way. If a stakeholder is naturally inclined another way, you will probably think they are being difficult – in fact they are responding normally for someone of their type. Once you are aware of this, it's much easier to deal with others effectively. Their behaviour becomes natural rather than provocative. You can work together rather than in conflict. If you can, take a full profile, like the Myers-Briggs Type Profile or the Insights Colour Wheel. Get a feel for different personality types and how you react to them. Be prepared to counter your natural reaction.

Outcome Awareness of your inclinations will prevent irritation because someone else is different, and hence stop negotiations snarling up over personalities.

Variations It's rarely possible for everyone in a negotiation to take a profile, but you could see if the other stakeholders are aware of their own profile.

Strategic   ✪✪✪✪
Intuitive   ✪✪✪
Process   ✪✪✪
Fun   ✪✪

5.42 | **Wooing them**

Preparation None.
Running time Two minutes.
Resources Pen and paper.
Timing Once.

No one is going to cave in and let you have your own way in a negotiation just because you buy them a meal or smile at them – but there is no doubt, even though everyone is aware of what is happening, that such wooing does soften up the resistance of the stakeholders. Spend two minutes listing different ways you can woo other parties in a negotiation. Try to be as creative as possible (see *Creative negotiation*, 5.38). Don't go on to the feedback section until you have done this.

Feedback Such wooing is very much a matter of motivation (see the books in Chapter 6 on motivation, starting on page 126). Your aim is to motivate those involved to be more inclined to go along with you. Hence, all the armoury of motivation is available to you. It might be a matter of reward or simply demonstrating trust. It might involve extra communication or giving them more room for manoeuvre. The art of motivation is manipulating people in such a way that they don't feel they are being manipulated but actively enjoy it.

In practical terms, you might use going for a drink or a meal to motivate. It may involve being socially charming. It could involve being considerate. For instance, you might know that some stakeholders have young children. You could suggest an early finish to the negotiation so that they could see their children before bedtime. (Such an approach has to be used with care to avoid sounding patronizing.) You can also look at the shape of the negotiating session. Some aspects of negotiation are relatively light, others hard work. Some are enjoyable, some depressing. If you can orchestrate the session so that the good parts come before natural breaks (particularly lunch and the end of the day), you can send the other stakeholders out feeling positive, rather than brooding over their difficulties. Wooing at its most subtle.

Outcome Building up your motivational skills will strongly benefit your ability to negotiate.

Variations None.

Strategic ✪✪✪
Intuitive ✪✪✪✪
Process ✪✪
Fun ✪✪✪

5.43 | *Selling your wider strengths*

Preparation None.
Running time 10 minutes.
Resources Pen and paper.
Timing Once.

Imagine that you are applying for a job. Thanks to excellent intelligence, you find out about all the other applicants. There are three others, each with exactly the same qualifications, experience and skills as you. There is nothing to choose between you on the area of the job itself.

Spend five minutes establishing what your wider strengths are. What sells you as an individual other than the specific experience and skills associated with your job? Spend a further five minutes looking at how you would use those wider strengths to sell yourself. How would you link them to the needs of the job and the company? How would you emphasize just how important these wider strengths are? What lessons for your work area can be drawn from the areas where your wider strengths apply?

Feedback At first sight this hasn't a lot to do with negotiation, but bear in mind that a lot of negotiation is about selling your side of the deal (even if the negotiation is actually about buying). Part of the preparation for a negotiation ought to be an exploration of wider strengths, and tying them back to the main requirement, just as you did in exercise 5.43. It needn't take much longer than the 10 minutes you took, but it can have immense value. Don't overlook strengths that don't seem to have a lot to do with the deal – as you (hopefully) saw in your own case, the impact of diversity is the whole point.

Outcome Giving thought to wider strengths and using them to influence a negotiation can tip the balance where the other stakeholders have little reason for making a choice. The more you can look out for wider strengths and their application, the better chance you have.

Variations If you have recently undertaken a negotiation, or are about to soon, take a few minutes to check out your wider strengths.

Strategic   ✪
Intuitive   ✪✪
Process   ✪
Fun   ✪✪

5.44 | **Common ground**

Preparation None.
Running time 10 minutes.
Resources Web access.
Timing Once.

Find the Web site of a political party that you would not normally support (a few example sites are listed below). Spend a few minutes browsing through their policies. Suspend any partisan feelings and look for the policies that you, as an individual, think are sensible. Think of the separate policies without any of the baggage and associations that they would normally carry. Note these common-ground points down.

* Conservative Party (UK) – **www.conservative.org.uk**
* Labour Party (UK) – **www.labour.org.uk**
* Liberal Democrats (UK) – **www.libdems.org.uk**
* Democrats (US) – **www.democrat.org**
* Republicans (US) – **www.rnc.org**

Feedback It is very easy to slip into partisan mode, where everything you think and say is right, and everything 'they' think and say is wrong. The more that you can get on the same side of the table as the other stakeholders, the better the chance of attaining a win–win outcome. As part of your preparation for a negotiation, look for your areas of common ground. When you are negotiating, don't dismiss all the other stakeholders' viewpoints – again, look for points of common ground.

Outcome Elements of common ground can be used to build trust and enhance your prospects of a win–win outcome. We get into a habitual state of assuming that we are diametrically at odds with the other stakeholders where often there is significant overlap. By practising to find common ground in politics, another area where overlap is often ignored, you can improve your chances of getting it right in negotiation.

Variations Another resource that is very useful for the 'common-ground' exercise is a TV political broadcast by a party that you would not normally support, again looking for the common ground.

Strategic	✪✪✪
Intuitive	✪✪✪
Process	✪
Fun	✪✪

5.45 | *Rehearsing for success*

Preparation None.
Running time Variable.
Resources None.
Timing Regularly.

Like all human interaction skills, negotiation benefits hugely from practice. Whatever your aims in improving your negotiation, you will have regular opportunities to practise in real life. Make something of these opportunities with a three-point plan.

1. Spot the opportunities. Often your chances to practise get missed. Look out for any major purchases, changes in your job, dealing with service companies, etc.

2. Treat the opportunity as a true negotiation. Put in more homework than you normally would, because this is now a learning process as well as a simple transaction. Use any of the *Instant Negotiation* techniques you have already mastered, and be prepared to throw in a few new ones that seem to fit particularly well.

3. Have a post-mortem (either alone or with a mentor) after the negotiation. Look out for occasions when you gave something away or missed something. From each 'rehearsal' negotiation pick out two or three key points for improvement.

Feedback Many of the exercises in *Instant Negotiation* are slightly removed from the actual negotiation process. They help to bolster skills that will benefit your next negotiation. But it would be a terrible waste to let real negotiations slip by without using them as on-the-ground training. All too often when we make a purchase or participate in a simple, day-to-day negotiation we assume that there is no room for movement. That's hardly ever the case. Remember all those possible variables. Why are you letting the other stakeholders set everything? Get yourself a better deal – and learn from your mistakes as well.

Outcome You can't beat practical application to test and refine people skills. This approach gives you a relatively safe testing ground on which to try out your negotiation skills.

Variations None.

Strategic ✪✪✪✪
Intuitive ✪
Process ✪✪✪✪
Fun ✪✪✪

5.46 | *Yes... eventually*

Preparation None.
Running time Two minutes.
Resources None.
Timing Several times.

It is in the nature of negotiating that there are no fixed rules, but a principle that comes close to being a rule is that you should never say 'yes' first time. It's the inverse of the concept that everything is negotiable – so to say 'yes' to whatever is first on offer is simply missing the opportunities to negotiate.

The chances that the starting conditions are exactly how you want things to be are negligible – and you will normally be able to lose something you don't want to gain something you do. There's not much of an exercise here, except to bear this in mind each time you negotiate. It's not a matter of being nasty or negative – just don't rush in and agree without getting some benefit. As an exercise, monitor the next few discussions you have and watch out for the over-eager 'yes'.

Feedback   You may not have major negotiations every day, but this is an exercise you can practise in many dealings with other people. It may not be a good idea for your day-to-day social interactions with family and friends, but bear in mind next time you buy something for the house, or a member of staff wants to talk about a pay rise.

One way to avoid sounding negative as a result of this policy is make sure that you are very open and positive about agreeing with anything that isn't setting a variable. Plenty of 'Yes, you're right' and nodding when they are discussing how great their company is (or whatever) will stand you in good stead when you don't say 'yes' to their first offer.

Outcome   This is a balancing exercise. A number of other exercises encourage you to take a positive and likeable attitude to the other stakeholders. With this balance, you can stay positive but not give too much away.

Variations   None.

Strategic	✪
Intuitive	✪✪
Process	✪✪
Fun	✪✪

5.47 | *Little successes*

Preparation None.
Running time Two minutes.
Resources None.
Timing Several times.

This technique, developed from one in *Instant Stress Management* (see page 127), is ideal to help with a long-term negotiation where you don't seem to be getting anywhere. Self-esteem is an important contributory factor to stress management. If your self-esteem is low, you are much more likely to succumb to stress-related illness. One of the undermining factors that keeps self-esteem low is the diminishing spiral that says 'I never achieve anything' – you feel bad about not achieving, so you get stressed and achieve even less.

This is a very quick exercise that can have a surprisingly powerful effect on self-esteem. Spend a couple of minutes jotting down a handful of small achievements you have made in the day. However bad a day you've had, you should be able to find something positive to say – force yourself to generate at least three; don't take 'no' for an answer. Repeat this exercise each day for a week or two.

Feedback Negotiation can be damaging to your self-esteem. Day after day you sit and talk and seem to get nowhere. By using this technique you can boost your self-esteem and ensure that you can continue negotiation in a positive frame of mind. Stick to small achievements for this exercise. No one is going to have a big achievement every day, but we all have some small achievements that will prove the fictional nature of the destructive view that you never succeed at anything.

Outcome It might seem that such a small success – it might just be 'I got to work on time' or 'I told my children a bedtime story' – is small beer compared to your bogged-down negotiations. It doesn't matter; much of the stress from lack of self-esteem derives from an imagined bleak picture that 'everything' goes wrong for you. Realistically this can't be true – and proving it to yourself will help.

Variations You could do this on a day-by-day basis, or (perhaps better) accumulate a list of all the little plusses across the period of your negotiation.

Strategic ✪
Intuitive ✪✪✪✪
Process ✪✪✪✪
Fun ✪✪✪

5.48 | *Slowing the pace*

Preparation None.
Running time Five minutes.
Resources None.
Timing Once.

In undertaking a negotiation, you are normally aiming for a particular goal. It's only human to want to reach that goal as soon as possible. In fact, you want it now. So it's a natural tendency to rush things to get finished. Unless there's an overriding time pressure, resist this urge. Slow down. This has two beneficial effects. It gives you a chance to get your facts right, to ensure that you say and do the right things. The more you are rushed, the more likely you are to make a mistake. And also slowing down will put the pressure to move on to the other stakeholders. Seeing that you aren't in any hurry might force their hands.

For this exercise, spend five minutes thinking about how you control the pace of a negotiation or other discussion. You can explicitly slow things down, or introduce secondary factors that result in a more measured pace. You can pause to think. You can arrange breaks and timeouts. That's just a sample. Get together a 'slowing down' toolkit that you can have alongside you. All you need to do now is to observe the pace of negotiation when it is taking place, and be prepared to employ that toolkit.

Feedback Sometimes there is a real time pressure, but often timing is a much more arbitrary input to the process than might seem to be the case. Identify where time pressures are coming from and separate the immovable from the other stakeholders' desires. There's something strange happening here. After all, the argument is that slowing things down gives you a chance to be more considered – but it seems to have the opposite effect on the stakeholders, who will come under pressure as a result of the timing. The reason for this paradoxical outcome is that the slowing down is under your control – so can simultaneously help you and hinder others.

Outcome Slowing things down will give you a chance to put your input in safely and may push other stakeholders into movement.

Variations None.

Strategic	✪
Intuitive	✪✪✪
Process	✪✪✪
Fun	✪✪

5.49 | *Throwing in the condiment*

Preparation None.
Running time 10 minutes.
Resources None.
Timing Once.

Once upon a time, when you stayed in a bed and breakfast in the UK you were charged extra for 'Use of cruet' – the salt, pepper, vinegar and sauces. This use of a small charge on the side for something everyone wants is still widely used to bump up income, if not in the hotel trade any more. A related approach can be used in negotiation to move things in your direction.

What the condiment can do for your negotiation is not so much to add a little income as to generate a new set of levers. If you can split off small elements of the cost as separate packages, you can then throw those back into the deal as a bargaining chip. 'If you can give us a guaranteed order for two years, we'll cover the packaging cost', or 'If you can see your way to doubling the order, we won't need to charge for either the pre-installation checks or the first year's servicing'.

Spend 10 minutes thinking about your products and services and identifying the condiments – the small items that are essential to the overall requirement, but can be separated off as an individual charge.

Feedback   The great thing about this approach is that you can generate movement from nothing, because you never intended to charge for the condiment elements in the first place. Make sure that there aren't too many and they are all known upfront. There is nothing worse than a whole page full of add-on costs, or costs that are only revealed late in the day.

Outcome   By dropping various near-fictional condiment costs you can achieve a considerable amount in return.

Variations   None.

Strategic ✪
Intuitive ✪
Process   ✪✪✪
Fun   ✪✪

5.50 | *Deadlines – the movable feast*

Preparation None.
Running time Five minutes.
Resources Pen and paper.
Timing Once.

Your deadlines are an effective way of adding leverage to your negotiation; the other stakeholders' deadlines are almost always subject to movement. Of course, a moment's thought suggests that this is an unsustainable difference – but only if the other stakeholders are as good at negotiating as you are, and it's always worth a try. Consider each of these four scenarios and how you would handle the deadline.

1. You have a meeting room booked in a hotel. The hotel has stated that you should be out by 5pm. By mid-afternoon it becomes clear that you are unlikely to be finished before 7pm. What do you do?

2. You are told 'My boss has given me authority to offer this price, but only for today'. You want to wait until the end of the week to check out some alternatives. What do you do?

3. You want to make sure a sale goes through before the end of the month. How do you encourage the buyer to stick to the deadline?

4. You want to make sure a debtor pays up by the end of the month. How do you encourage them to do so while maintaining good relations (you expect future business)?

Feedback As always with such examples, these aren't the only answers – the main point is that you think about the implications of deadlines. If you haven't had a go yourself, jot down some answers before continuing.

In the first example, it makes sense to explain your predicament to the hotel and ask nicely – often they will extend the period. If they become difficult, point out that you had hoped to use them for a series of meetings, but if they can't deal with this sort of flexibility... (you may need to speak to the manager to use this approach). For the second example, you might be near conspiratorial. 'I really want to go with this offer, but I can't do anything until the end of the week. Could we call up your boss – I'd be happy to speak to her, and it'd be a shame for both of us to miss out on a great business opportunity because of red tape.'

There are, of course, many ways to encourage a sale to happen by a certain time. The power of the printed word (see 5.15) means that you can use a price list with an expiry date to push for a sale before that date. You could also point out that you are expecting big orders next month, so it would be really good for the customer to be at the top of the priority list, before these big orders clog up the system. Or you could point out how circumstances beyond your control (the tax man, your suppliers) are forcing you to put prices up after that date.

The tax man is also a good ally in encouraging a late payer. It's probably best not to resort to threats if this isn't likely to be a repeated problem and you want a long-term relationship. Instead, highlight how damaging it is to you (you've big bills to cover, you need the cash to ensure their next order is processed on time, and so on).

Outcome   Deadlines can be an irritation or a lever. Playing the deadlines game is rather like noughts and crosses (tic-tac-toe). At worst it will result in a draw, but you may catch your opponent off-guard and win advantage.

Variations   None.

Strategic	✪
Intuitive	✪✪✪
Process	✪✪✪
Fun	✪✪

5.51 | *Remote negotiation*

Preparation None.
Running time Five minutes.
Resources E-mail, stooge.
Timing Once.

Modern communications mean that it is possible to conduct a negotiation without ever seeing the other stakeholders. Generally speaking this is not a good idea for a major negotiation, but is fine for many smaller-scale negotiations.

The two prime possibilities are the telephone and e-mail. Phone-based negotiations are the weakest of all options. You lack much of the sub-text of a face-to-face meeting, and it is simply too easy to hang up. E-mail, on the other hand, has some real benefits for low-value negotiation. It automatically introduces the authority of the written word, and can provide worldwide negotiation despite time zones. In an e-mail you can propose a movement and give all the supporting argument before the other stakeholder gets a chance to counter-propose.

Get a colleague to help out in an e-mail negotiation exercise. Imagine you wanted to sell a PC or a car. Your colleague should play an interested buyer – someone who definitely wants what you've got for sale, but nonetheless intends to get the best deal they can. Undertake an e-mail negotiation. You might like then to try reversing the exercise, with your colleague trying to sell you something different.

Feedback   In doing the exercise, aim to make the best of the medium, using its strengths to get your message across. Don't just type and send off an e-mail. Reread it a couple of times, polishing it up as you go. I must reiterate that face to face is always best for significant negotiations, but e-mail has generated a very effective niche in these smaller concerns.

Outcome   With e-mail added to your negotiating armoury you can take on a broader scope of negotiations – or use e-mail to encourage between-sessions movement in a major negotiation.

Variations   As always, a simulation is no substitute for the real thing. If any opportunity arises for a real online negotiation, try it out.

Strategic	✪✪
Intuitive	✪✪
Process	✪
Fun	✪✪

5.52 | *Make them feel good about the deal*

Preparation None.
Running time Two minutes.
Resources None.
Timing Once.

Ideally, although you are aiming for win–win, you want to have done the best possible deal while still leaving the other stakeholders feeling that they've achieved something. You might think that once the deal is signed and sealed, this obligation no longer applies – but beware.

Imagine the situation. You've just closed a negotiation successfully and take your team for a drink at a local bar. In come the other stakeholders. 'Wow', you say to them, 'We walked all over you. You didn't know what hit you, did you? We would have paid twice as much if you'd kept going there.'

What happens? You feel briefly elated at showing the other side just how well you beat them. They feel dejected and upset. When they get back to the office they will do all they can to get back at you. They'll try to sabotage this deal, and if they can't, they will certainly make sure you have trouble with them in the future. An expensive moment's crowing. Leave triumphant posturing to soap operas – make sure your last few minutes contact with the other stakeholders leaves them feeling buoyed and successful.

Feedback If you want to tell them anything, tell them how they slaughtered you. Not only will they feel good about it, they might be more lenient in the future. It's human nature that you will celebrate once you are on your own; however, in the event of the other stakeholders walking in on your celebration, make sure that you put it across as a celebration of mutual success – and invite them to join in.

Outcome It might seem that you are buttering up someone who has just lost out to you – but you can afford to be magnanimous in such circumstances, and the fact is that you are more likely to get good business in the future this way.

Variations None.

Strategic ✪✪✪✪
Intuitive ✪✪✪✪
Process ✪
Fun ✪

5.53 | *Plotting the journey*

Preparation None.
Running time 15 minutes.
Resources Pen, large sheet of paper.
Timing Once.

Imagine that you wanted to be the chief executive of a large company. If you work for a large company (and you aren't already in that position), use your own. Otherwise pick a well-known corporate giant. Let's say you gave yourself 10 years to get there.

On a piece of paper sketch out a map from here to there. Use the paper sideways (landscape). Put your present position at the left-hand edge, with the chief executive position at the right-hand edge. Draw a line linking them. On the line, sketch in a number of milestones – intermediate positions you might take stock of. They can be time-based, or based on clearly different responsibilities between your current position and the goal. Around the starting point, note down what things are like now; what skills and experience you have.

Finally, along the route, sketch in any potential obstacles. If possible, write a few options for overcoming them.

Feedback   This example intentionally takes a step back from the negotiation process, but such a map of a negotiation is valuable in two ways. It helps you to plan out your tactics, and it can be used during the negotiation period to plot progress and keep you aware of potential obstacles. By using a long-term goal in the exercise (the chief executive's job), the need for establishing milestones along the way and looking out for obstacles becomes clearer – but they are just as important in a day's negotiation. This isn't a tool for use at the negotiating table, but rather on your home territory when planning or regrouping. To be able to draw a map, you need to know where you are going. This exercise is a good follow-on from *Which way?*, 5.33.

Outcome   On any complex journey a map is valuable. All but the most simple of negotiations will benefit from one.

Variations   If you have a real long-term goal in mind (giving up smoking, becoming a millionaire... anything), try doing a map like this for real.

Strategic ✪✪✪✪
Intuitive ✪✪
Process ✪✪✪✪
Fun ✪✪✪

5.54 | *Using silence*

Preparation None.
Running time 15 minutes.
Resources Stooge.
Timing Once.

For this exercise you need a stooge who is unaware of your intentions. The aim is to get some practice at using silence. Get into conversation with a friend or colleague, in a situation where you would expect to chat for 20 minutes or so. This exercise won't work if either of you is in a hurry. Once the conversation has got going, start to use silence consciously. When the other person has said something, don't jump in. Instead, look fascinated. You might nod or smile or make a 'hmm' noise for encouragement, but try to force the stooge to continue by using only silence. You may find this difficult at first – work at it. You will have to be unusually careful about your expression, to ensure that you don't come across as bored (or vacant), without appearing to suffer from painful facial contortions.

Feedback Silence is one of the negotiator's best weapons, yet it is rarely used to full effect. Most of us find it embarrassing to remain silent for long. We feel the urge to jump in and fill the gap. When we do so, we let the other stakeholders off the hook. They too feel the need to say something – so give them a chance.

Just occasionally you will hit a Mexican standoff, where everyone involved is good at handling silence, and the lack of input becomes silly. If nothing has been said at all for five minutes, it might be worth speaking. But not to give anything away. Say something like 'I think we're getting bogged down here. We could all do with some fresh air. I suggest we have a five-minute stretch break.' Or words to that effect.

Outcome Getting some practice at overcoming the embarrassment of silence is important if you are going to use it effectively. Otherwise, no matter what your intention, you will cave in and speak.

Variations It would be best if you could undertake this exercise in a natural social meeting, rather than an engineered one, which may make you feel even more uncomfortable. The exercise has to be one to one – if there are other people in the conversation, they will do the leaping in, and silence will no longer be in use.

Strategic	✪
Intuitive	✪✪✪
Process	✪
Fun	✪

5.55 | *Cornered rats*

Preparation None.
Running time Five minutes.
Resources None.
Timing Once.

Spend a few minutes thinking about negotiations you have been involved with. They could be the formal negotiations of business, or the (more frequent) social negotiations from 'What shall we have for dinner?' to 'Where shall we go on holiday?' List a handful of negotiations where both sides have backed themselves into a corner and been unable to move. What happened? How did you feel? How did you get out of the deadlock?

Feedback All too often you can reach a point where all the stakeholders have no room for manoeuvre. Immediately, what could have been a very amicable negotiation passes into something closer to warfare. In fact, actual warfare is generally generated by just such conditions. The best cure is to avoid it happening in the first place. If you see the possibility looming, take a step to try to stay on the same side. Bring the potential deadlock explicitly into the conversation and look for ways to avoid it.

Failing that, a brief cooling-off period is usually valuable. Once you have dug yourselves into your respective positions you won't be in any mood for compromise. Step back from the negotiation for a while. When you return, don't keep on the same line, only look at places where there is a chance for movement. Make sure you are working together in partnership, rather than against each other (at least until you are out of the hole). Phrase your language inclusively and positively – make it all about 'we', not 'you', and solutions, not problems.

Outcome Your own practical experience of deadlocks will come in very useful; don't waste it – build on it.

Variations None.

Strategic ✪
Intuitive ✪✪✪
Process ✪✪✪
Fun ✪✪

5.56 | **Ask, ask and ask again**

Preparation None.
Running time Two minutes.
Resources None.
Timing Regularly.

You go to a potential major customer and attempt a negotiation. The outcome is negative. They decide to go elsewhere (or not to go ahead at all). So what do you? Go and find another customer. That's great, but there's more to do. Go back to the first customer at a later date.

This is a very quick technique, but always worth doing. Each time you have a breakdown in a sales negotiation, make a note to go back. The exact period of time will depend on your business – but it might be in a month or two or even six. The important thing is to make a note in your diary so that at the end of that period you go back to see if it is possible to revisit the negotiation, or a new opportunity. And keep it up in good Robert the Bruce fashion.

Feedback   It might seem that you are beating your head against a brick wall, but circumstances change. The people you are dealing with move on. Monies become available. Competitors go away. Revisiting the stakeholders of an old failed negotiation requires much less effort than starting again from scratch, so even if you only achieve a breakthrough once every hundred times, it's probably cost effective (if demotivating).

Outcome   Going back and revisiting failed sales negotiations will get you extra business at a relatively low cost.

Variations   None.

Strategic ✪✪✪✪
Intuitive ✪
Process ✪✪✪✪
Fun ✪

5.57 | *Coffee and doughnuts*

Preparation None.
Running time 15 minutes.
Resources None.
Timing Regularly.

If you're a manager and want to improve your leadership skills, a highly recommended technique is to have regular coffee and doughnuts sessions (at your expense) with your staff. It's a chance to speak informally, often about matters totally unconnected with work. The main benefit of the coffee and doughnuts sessions if done right is to move from 'them and us' to just 'us'. It helps to get everyone on the same side.

In a negotiation you are faced with a group of people you might not know particularly well. Even in a fact-finding negotiation you will often find yourselves on different sides of an issue, while in a selling negotiation this is inevitable. So why not take a mid-morning break or mid-afternoon break for coffee and doughnuts? Force the conversation away from the negotiation. Give yourself a few minutes to establish that the others taking part are people, not automata. Maybe even people you quite like. It's worth the cost of a few doughnuts.

Feedback The doughnuts (or some other fancy snacks) are important. Coffee alone, or even coffee and biscuits, is too institutionalized a concept. The idea of the doughnuts is to make it more of a social affair, more of a treat. You may find that other stakeholders try to move the conversation back to the negotiation. Unless there are special circumstances, resist this. Don't be brusque, but say something like, 'I don't know about you, but there are times when I just need to clear my head a bit'. Then lead on to ask them about their weekend or some other harmless topic.

Outcome The coffee and doughnuts session has a double benefit. It gives you a chance to establish more of a rapport with the other negotiators, and it provides a break in your work. All too often negotiations can get bogged down with hour after hour of talks. As you spend longer and longer in a session your effectiveness and productivity plummets. A chance to do something completely different will revive your input, too.

Variations None.

Strategic	✪
Intuitive	✪✪✪✪
Process	✪✪✪
Fun	✪✪✪✪

5.58 | *Body language*

Preparation Find a stooge.
Running time 10 minutes.
Resources Video camera.
Timing Once.

Your body language will always contribute to the quality of your negotiation. Try this little exercise. Get someone else to act as a participant in a tough negotiation. Video a few minutes discussion as you argue the fact that you can't go any cheaper, while the stooge tries to beat down your price. Lie blatantly.

Now check out the video. Look for any signs of closing up – crossing your arms, curling up on the chair, avoiding eye contact and so forth. Similarly look for occasions when you are open and warm.

The point of this exercise is to be aware of what your body language is like, so that you can do something about it in a real negotiation. Some of your body language will result from the artificial nature of the situation, but it should still be an effective guide.

Feedback I am not suggesting that you lie blatantly in real negotiations, but by forcing yourself to lie you are more likely to indulge in the sort of negative body language that could come out in the pressures of a normal negotiation.

Be conscious of your body language when negotiating. Make sure that you use open positions more – sitting back, arms apart, open-handed, smiling, looking the other stakeholders in the eye. Before long it will seem quite natural, even if it feels very uncomfortable at first.

Outcome By employing more open body language, even under stress, you will come across as honest and positive. Don't let your body give the game away or, even worse, misrepresent your stress as dishonesty.

Variations None.

Strategic ✪✪✪
Intuitive ✪✪✪✪
Process ✪
Fun ✪✪

5.59 Don't leave the next step in their hands

Preparation None.
Running time 10 minutes.
Resources None.
Timing Once.

You've reached a stage in the negotiation where the other stakeholders need to withdraw. Perhaps they have to go back to base and talk. Maybe they're just embarrassed about counting on their fingers in front of you. Whatever reason, the negotiation is temporarily suspended. There's danger lurking here. When the others get back to their normal environment they may be distracted. Keep them on track. The same day as the negotiation ends, drop them a note, stating positively what has been agreed so far.

So often, letters like this end with something like, 'Thanks for taking the time to discuss the matter with us – if you'd like to take it further, please get in touch.' Sounds harmless? It's not, because you have just relinquished control. Instead, say something like, 'I'll be back to you in a week's time to fix up the next session', or whatever is appropriate. Keep the initiative and move the process forward. It only takes a few minutes to send a letter like this and follow it up – but it can be a very valuable few minutes.

Spend 10 minutes thinking through the tasks and activities you are currently involved in. How many of them are out of your control? What could you do to get them moving?

Feedback I don't quite know why, but it's difficult to keep the reins in this way. Perhaps it feels as if you are being pushy. But without it, you have lost control of the process. Be sensitive to the other stakeholders' reactions. If, for instance, when you ring up they are evasive about fixing a date to get together, say something like, 'You are obviously very busy now. Can I call you again in a week and see how things are going?' Again, you've kept the initiative. Don't let go.

Outcome The chances of reaching a successful conclusion to your negotiations are crucially dependent on keeping in control.

Variations None.

Strategic ✪✪
Intuitive ✪
Process ✪✪✪
Fun ✪✪

5.60 | *Say what?*

Preparation None.
Running time 10 minutes.
Resources Pen and paper.
Timing Once.

Achieving clarity in what you say will almost always help in negotiating. Unless you are intentionally setting out to befuddle the other stakeholders – generally a high-risk option – clarity will ensure that there is the minimum confusion on the way to an outcome.

Spend five minutes writing a reasonably detailed description of one of your products or services, or something else about which you are likely to have a negotiation. Don't go any further until you have written it.

When you have written your piece, go back over it taking the viewpoint of your grandmother, or someone from another planet who only understands basic English. How much have you resorted to jargon? Sometimes it easy to do so without even realizing that the words you have used are jargon. Go over it word for word with a fine toothcomb.

Feedback You can do this with written documents in real negotiations, but you will have to be more careful with the spoken word. Try to monitor what you are saying, keeping an ear out for jargon. If possible, have a colleague listen to what you say.

In some ways negotiation is a very strange form of communication. Whereas in conventional communication you are in the business of revealing, in negotiation there is always an element of concealment. Your intention is to keep your cards close to your chest until it's time to reveal them. Many of them you hope you will never have to reveal. But that doesn't mean that what you do say should be incomprehensible or misleading. It can only result in confusion.

Outcome Reducing jargon in your communication will increase the chances of understanding and a win–win outcome.

Variations Jargon is essentially a shorthand technique for communication between those in the know. If everyone present is familiar with it, it can be employed – but beware local variations in jargon that will lead to confusion.

Strategic	✪
Intuitive	✪
Process	✪
Fun	✪✪

5.61 | **You won't win them all**

Preparation None.
Running time Evening.
Resources Expenses.
Timing After failed negotiation.

This is a special exercise, as it should only be undertaken after a negotiation has failed. You will be feeling down. You could have won, but you didn't. We're not talking here about giving way on a few variables, but total collapse of the negotiation. No deal. Perhaps a competitor has walked all over you.

You could go into a corner and sulk, but it won't do you any good. Instead, consider having a wake. Celebrate the collapse of the negotiation and what you've learned from it (make sure you do learn something from it).

If it's a big negotiation, go out for a meal or go to a show. Otherwise, you might celebrate by getting yourself a small treat. Whatever you do, though, do it with the intent of burying the failure and moving on. Celebrate in the knowledge that next morning you are going to start something even better – and make sure that you do make a start.

Feedback This isn't hiding your head in the sand. You have failed, and it is bound to be disappointing. After all, unless you go into a negotiation knowing that you are going to win, you are handicapping yourself with your own inability. But there is no benefit to be had from wallowing in the misery that can accompany failure. There are three key elements here: learning from the failure; giving the negotiation a send-off celebration; and moving quickly on, ideally to something bigger and better.

Outcome There will be failures. Everyone has them. But coping effectively with failures is essential if you are going to be successful as a negotiator.

Variations None.

Strategic ✪✪✪✪
Intuitive ✪✪✪
Process ✪✪✪✪
Fun ✪✪✪✪

5.62 | *Principles*

Preparation None.
Running time Five minutes.
Resources Notebook or sheet of paper.
Timing Once.

Time management has some essential lessons for negotiators. Some time management gurus recommend having a mission statement, but I find they make me nauseous. It's important to know what you like doing, and are good at, and to have a set of focal activities that are the most important things for you to be doing. However, there is something else: the underlying principles driving these activities. Your focal activities are about what; your principles say why. Understanding your personal principles is a valuable tool in improving your negotiation skills – and sometimes in understanding why you will fail at a particular negotiation.

Be honest. Perhaps you do things for power, or to spend more time with your children. Perhaps you want fame or an easy life. Perhaps it's love of God or belief in humanity. Principles don't have to be deep, though. You might include: 'Have fun every day', or 'Don't worry about things you can't influence'. Clichés? Maybe, but clichés and fallacies are different: clichés are often true. Most people have three to six major principles driving their activities. Spend a few minutes pulling together what drives you. Stick them at the front of your notebook or on the wall.

Feedback Putting your principles on view has most impact, but they embarrass many people. It's an indictment of our society that we don't like to admit to such things. Hide them away if you like, but understand what you are doing, and why.

Outcome Your principles provide a fixed reference. When deciding on the tactics to use in negotiating, when evaluating your priorities, you don't need to read your principles every time, but they are there as a yardstick.

Variations Most principles are personal, but a few apply to most people. A particular favourite is the Pareto (or 80:20) rule that 80 per cent of the value can be gained from 20 per cent of the effort.

Strategic ✪✪✪✪
Intuitive ✪✪✪✪
Process ✪✪✪
Fun ✪✪

5.63 | *Aim high to get more*

Preparation None.
Running time 10 minutes.
Resources Pen and paper.
Timing Once.

Look at the prices of a couple of your products and services (or equivalent). For each, jot down at least three good reasons for doubling the price. Now consider any recent contracts. Again, jot down at least three good reasons for doubling the quantities involved.

Feedback Of course, in every instance there will be a hundred reasons why you shouldn't double the prices. All the competition are operating at about the same price. That's how things have always been priced. And so on. But maybe you have been looking at the wrong competition. Maybe what you have to offer is so much better than that of the opposition that it's worth twice the price. There are always arguments for aiming high – bear in mind also that you will have to sell less to make the same amount of money. Of course, you still have to sell some. There is a balance. But you don't get anywhere by underselling yourself.

You can see some of this happening in *Starting prices*, 5.23, but I wanted to pull it out as an exercise in its own right because it's a fundamental issue that goes across the whole of negotiating, not just starting prices. You will fail more if you aim high, and you need to support that high aim with great follow through – it's no use bidding for a contract that's way out of your league and not fulfilling it – but aiming high is the only way you can rise above the rest. It is worth the risk.

Outcome Aiming high is necessary to exceed expectations. And if you don't exceed expectations, you will be never more than moderately regarded or successful. No more to say.

Variations Try the same exercise, quadrupling the prices.

Strategic	✪✪
Intuitive	✪✪✪
Process	✪✪✪
Fun	✪✪

5.64 | *There's always an 'if'*

Preparation The agreement space (5.4).
Running time Five minutes.
Resources None.
Timing Once.

When negotiating it's easy to feel positive about the other people involved. That's good – you want them to like you, and that is often best achieved by liking them back. But don't let this liking, or some obscure sense of chivalry, push you into the biggest mistake known to any negotiator. Don't forget the 'if'. Never give the other stakeholders anything for free – make them pay for it.

Say, for instance, they want you to cut your price, you can say 'I can see that would be advantageous, and it would be practical for me if we could up the order by 25 per cent'. Or you may be buying and the sellers say 'You'll have to wait four weeks for delivery'. Don't meekly take it between the eyes. Still be positive, but positively say, 'That's fine, if it's possible to throw in the maintenance for free, otherwise my cash flow is shot to pieces'. Or whatever.

Take the variables from *The agreement space*, 5.4. For each one, see if you can provide an 'if' – you would accept some movement in this variable if...

Feedback I don't really understand why, but there's often a lemming-like urge to give things away, sometimes when they're not even asked for. Guard against this. Make sure the 'if' or 'providing' is always there. That way, any negative movement is to some extent countered. Otherwise, you are simply indulging in charity.

Outcome 'If' is as powerful a two-letter word in negotiation as 'no' is in time management. Each can be surprisingly hard to use, but once you do, you are well on the way to success.

Variations None.

Strategic ✪
Intuitive ✪
Process ✪
Fun ✪✪

5.65 | Knowing your products and services

Preparation None.
Running time 15 minutes.
Resources Pen and paper.
Timing Once.

Sit down with a pen and paper, but none of your company's literature. On one sheet of paper, draw up a list of your key products and services. Group them into blocks, and for each block write a line or two that summarizes just what that group is about.

On a second piece of paper, pick out your company's highest money-making product or service. Make that single piece of paper a sales masterpiece. Describe the product or service and how it is used, but make the description as enticing as you can.

Feedback Many of us struggle with this exercise. We don't know enough without the sales literature to back us up. (Note, by the way, that this isn't just an exercise for salespeople, but for anyone who is going to negotiate for their company.) Ideally, you ought to be able to produce one of those detailed, exciting fact sheets for every major product and service. Perhaps it's time to do a little homework.

Knowing your company's range isn't just about getting the best deal on a specific product. It also makes it practical to bring other products and services into the deal and to sell a whole system, not just a product. The other stakeholders will want to see information on paper (see *The power of print*, 5.15), but they won't be impressed if you have to scramble through the printed material yourself to chase up a fact. It is also useful if you are buying as well as selling – after all, each vendor is also a potential customer.

Outcome Knowing your products and services is a fundamental requirement if you are to negotiate on behalf of your company.

Variations See *Knowing the opposition*, 5.30, for the other side of the requirement.

Strategic	✪
Intuitive	✪
Process	✪✪✪
Fun	✪✪

5.66 | *Doing a special*

Preparation None.
Running time Five minutes.
Resources None.
Timing Once.

Every now and then there's a need for a little push to get a negotiation over the final hurdle. If you are involved in selling, you might have use for this technique.

You have announced your 'final' price. The buyer says that she can't go that far for apparently legitimate reasons. You feel that a small price reduction (well within your room for manoeuvre) should clinch the deal, but don't want to offer it as you feel that the buyer will want to go further. All the other variables have been explored. Where do you go? Think about it for a moment before proceeding.

Feedback A handy technique is to say 'I can't go any further – as I've said, this is my limit. But if I ring my boss, he might be able to give me another five per cent, provided you don't mind giving him an endorsement for the company. Would that be a problem?' You then ring the boss and leave them waiting a minute or two. Finally the boss rings back and OKs the deal.

This technique not only puts a clear bottom on your pricing, it has the sneaky advantage of putting you on the other stakeholder's side. It's no longer them versus you, but both of you versus the boss. They will have a sense of relief when they get the go ahead, even if it's for something they hadn't intended to accept. Manipulative? A trifle. I wouldn't overuse this technique. But it will help out when you need to go a little further without losing control of the process, as has been proved in many used car and replacement-windows sales.

Outcome Bringing in a special from the boss can often tip a teetering negotiation over the edge.

Variations Technically you don't have to bring in the boss on the phone, you could take note of a special offer or deal that hadn't been available upfront, but the power of this approach is in the psychological effect of anticipation during the delay.

Strategic   ✪
Intuitive   ✪✪✪
Process   ✪✪
Fun   ✪✪

5.67 | *Slicing the salami*

Preparation Price wide range of items.
Running time Five minutes.
Resources Pen and paper.
Timing Once.

Get together the prices of a range of items from the very expensive (houses, helicopters, yachts), through mid-priced (cars, PCs) to household goods. Consider in each case what is the percentage discount that would make it worth spending an extra half hour negotiating.

Feedback There are two outcomes from this exercise. One is to make you more aware of the subjective way we regard pricing. It is unlikely that you will have been consistent on the cost you put on your time. You might be prepared to negotiate for £30 on a fridge, but not bother with less than £500 on a house. But it also reveals some of the salami slicing of price you are likely to see in a negotiation.

Generally speaking, if you are selling you need to be driving those slices down in size, getting down to the minimum that sounds as if it is delivering something. However, bear in mind the advice in *Price movement*, 5.75, about decreasing the size of price cuts over time, so it appears that you are heading for a point beyond which you can't go. You need to leave enough room in the initial slice of the salami for reduction in the future.

Outcome Overcoming your naturally illogicality over the impact of different slice sizes when dealing with different amounts, and managing to keep slices to the minimum effective size will help to keep your price movement to a minimum.

Variations None.

Strategic	✪
Intuitive	✪
Process	✪✪✪
Fun	✪✪

5.68 | **Walkies!**

Preparation Find location.
Running time 15 minutes.
Resources Suitable footwear.
Timing Regularly.

Go for a walk. End of technique.

Well, almost. This technique, derived from one in *Instant Stress Management* (see page 127), has more to it than that. Most physical exercise provides good stress relief, but walking scores especially highly. It isn't challenging, it doesn't make you look odd, and unlike most exercise it isn't mind-numbingly boring. Physical exercise is particularly important if you have been stuck all day round a negotiating table. Getting out into fresh air and letting your mind roam free will enhance your performance and reduce the chances that negotiating will be bad for your health.

If possible, walk somewhere where you can take in the natural stress relief of the countryside – fresh air, greenery, lack of traffic. But if you can't get to the countryside, at least get outside. Remember to use suitable footwear – trainers might not be your usual style, but they're much better than typical office shoes.

Feedback There are two approaches to stress-relief walking. You can either deliberately keep all your thoughts at bay, or let them work through. In the first approach, focus on your surroundings. Don't let your thoughts wander back to the negotiation. Imagine you are an artist or writer or composer and want to capture your surroundings – drink them in. If there are people around, take an interest in them (not too obviously) – everyone is interesting. The alternative approach is to let the negotiation and any surrounding facts slosh about in your mind. Don't make a heavy effort to find a solution – let things happen at their own pace.

Outcome Walking gives you the triple benefit of exercise, fresh air and an opportunity for your mind to work on the negotiation in a very different way. As an added bonus, it's a defence against stressors because you're usually out of reach (don't take your mobile). Make it happen.

Variations Fifteen minutes is a sensible minimum that you should be able to do several times a week – half an hour would be even better.

Strategic ✪✪
Intuitive ✪✪✪
Process ✪✪✪✪
Fun ✪✪✪✪

5.69 | *Good guy/bad guy*

Preparation None.
Running time Five minutes.
Resources None.
Timing As required.

Good guy/bad guy is one of the oldest negotiating techniques in the book. You have seen it many times in interrogation scenes in films. The heavy roughs the hero up, then the nice guy offers him a coffee and talks quietly and reasonably. And that's the trouble with this technique. We have all seen it before, we know it's happening and the connotations are negative in a big way. So don't do it.

But that doesn't mean you won't come up against it. Watch out for it – it is usually fairly obvious. When you are dealing with the bad guy, keep things light. Smile a lot. Let what is said wash over you with very little response. Bring up almost irrelevant points. If you are finding it really heavy going, resort to being slightly off the wall or personal – 'Did you choose that shirt yourself?' With the good guy press the advantage. Ignore everything the bad guy said, just pick up the good points and run with them, adding your own 'ifs' (see *There's always an 'if'*, 5.64).

Feedback It is probably better not to mention explicitly what is happening. The trouble is they usually won't admit to it and you are left feeling foolish. If you do decide to bring it above the counter, do so in such a way that doesn't give them a chance to argue. Like saying, 'I know you've been playing the nice guy/nasty guy game, but let's try it a different way; what if we…'.

Outcome By not using good guy/bad guy yourself you will have avoided giving yourself the wrong image. If you can then be aware of other stakeholders using this technique, you will be able to leverage it to your own advantage.

Variations None.

Strategic ✪
Intuitive ✪✪✪
Process ✪✪✪
Fun ✪✪✪

5.70 | *I haven't the authority...*

Preparation None.
Running time Two minutes.
Resources None.
Timing Once.

Imagine a confrontation between yourself as a buyer of replacement windows and yourself as a salesperson. With your buyer's hat on, you have said that you could only go ahead if given a 30 per cent price reduction. Your salesperson persona says that he or she hasn't got the authority. Work through the duel, taking one persona at a time. Challenge the salesperson's statement from the buyer's viewpoint, then find a way to counter the challenge. Keep going until you run out of steam.

Feedback The 'I haven't the authority' card is one you may wish to play – or to counter. This exercise gives experience of both. A possible dialogue might go:

Seller: I'm afraid I haven't got the authority to do that. Is there some other way we can sort it out?
Buyer: Who has the authority?
Seller: My manager, but he's in meetings all afternoon.
Buyer: Okay, when can I speak to him?
Seller: He is very busy this week.
Buyer: I'll see him next week.
Seller: This deal has to be completed before Friday.
Buyer: If time is that important, he'll spare me a minute. What's his number? ...etc.

Note the way that the buyer is always trying to take the initiative. The person trying to get out of a commitment should be careful not to get into a tangle (or even lie excessively) about someone else's availability. If possible have something in writing from your boss, making it clear that you can't go beyond a certain point. Try to move away from 'I want to talk to this person', 'I don't want you to'. Bring in other issues.

Outcome Whichever side you are on when the authority card is played, some degree of thinking through will help you to manage it better.

Variations None.

Strategic ✪
Intuitive ✪✪
Process ✪
Fun ✪✪

5.71 | **Appearing naïve**

Preparation None.
Running time Two minutes.
Resources None.
Timing Once.

This is an apparently simple technique that can be remarkably powerful. In a negotiation you may find that some points that the other stakeholders bring up are unacceptable. Rather than challenging them outright, use what politely could be described as a naïve response. (The less polite description is dumb.) Don't understand them. Admit to your stupidity and ask them to explain the point in more detail. Be prepared to do this several times. Try this out next time you are in a meeting and something is said that seems strange or incomprehensible.

Feedback To be successful with this technique you have to be without pride, because you have to admit to not understanding. In practice, this is something people should do a lot more of – if they did, there would be less disasters due to poor communication. But that isn't the reason for doing it.

As the other stakeholder has to expand on their point, a number of things can happen. It can be exposed as unsubstantiated. As he or she tries to justify it, it may be that a pit is dug that can't be escaped from. Alternatively, they could open up new variables. You might still not be able to do anything about this point, but the justification of the point might loosen up another point for movement. Or the repeated analysis of the point might encourage the stakeholder to give way. Even if there is no movement, you will have found out valuable information. But often an attack of naïvety can loosen up the arguments. And the great thing is, although you are effectively questioning the point, you are doing it in a non-aggressive way. You are admitting that you are being stupid about this, after all.

Outcome By seeming naïve you can achieve considerable movement without being threatening.

Variations This technique shouldn't be used too often or it will begin to seem to be a scheming tactic. It is a scheming tactic, but you don't want it to look like one!

Strategic	✪
Intuitive	✪✪
Process	✪
Fun	✪✪✪

5.72 | **Liking the opposition**

Preparation None.
Running time Five minutes.
Resources Pen and paper.
Timing Once.

Visualize someone you don't get on with particularly well. It could be someone at work or in the social environment. Spend a minute or two noting down just what it is that irritates you about them. Now put that to one side. Start noting down what is good about them. Everyone has a good side – bring it out. Everyone, however boring they appear superficially, is an individual human being with interests and is inherently interesting if you look at them in the right way. Get as much as you can down that is purely positive about this person. Given there is this positive side to them, consider whether you couldn't see ways of getting on a little better.

Feedback There's a natural tendency to be a bit suspicious about the other stakeholders in a negotiation. After all, they're out to get what they can and to screw you. (This might not be true, but it's often the working assumption.) It's easy to turn this into an actual dislike. This might not seem much of a problem – you are only trying to negotiate with the person, not date them. But your likes and dislikes will unconsciously colour your communication. If you like someone, you will come across as more positive. If you dislike them, you will come across as negative.

The outcome of these messages that you are sending is usually reciprocation. If you like someone, they will find it easier to like you. And the same goes for dislikes. If you want to achieve a win–win outcome, and to persuade the other stakeholders to come closer to your desired outcome, it's advantageous to like them. And while you can't absolutely force this, the technique in this exercise of looking for and mentally emphasizing the other person's good points will usually help in the process.

Outcome Liking is generally reciprocated, and will help in a win–win solution.

Variations None.

Strategic ✪✪✪
Intuitive ✪✪✪
Process   ✪✪✪
Fun   ✪✪✪

5.73 | **Stakeholder customer**

Preparation None.
Running time Five minutes.
Resources Pen and paper.
Timing Once.

Imagine for a moment that you are a small shopkeeper. Business is good, but a superstore is opening down the road that threatens to take away your customers. You decide that you are going to keep your customers (and even win new ones) by giving superb customer service. Spend five minutes putting together a checklist of the elements of great customer service. Not sure what this has to do with negotiating? Trust me.

Feedback Even when you aren't selling, there is a lot of similarity between the other stakeholders in a negotiation and customers. You want to win them over to your point of view; you want them to trust you. Look at your customer-service checklist and think how these elements could work in your favour. Bear in mind that treating a stakeholder like a customer doesn't mean giving them everything they want, but use the same techniques as you would use with a customer to get them on your side. Your list is probably the best one for you, but here are ten points from the book *Capturing Customers' Hearts* (see page 125 for details).

- Going out of your way to be helpful.
- Recovering generously from a mistake you make.
- Showing that you know the stakeholders and their needs.
- Using a star to head up the negotiation.
- Letting the stakeholders get to know you as a real, likeable person.
- Using positive surprises.
- Making the most of technical wizardry.
- Giving them some sense of ownership of your company.
- Keeping up good quality communications.
- Emphasizing your unique qualities and benefits.

Outcome If you can regard the other stakeholders as customers and treat them accordingly, you are much more likely to achieve a positive win–win outcome.

Variations None.

Strategic	✪✪✪✪
Intuitive	✪✪✪
Process	✪✪✪
Fun	✪✪✪

5.74 | *Being you*

Preparation None.
Running time Five minutes.
Resources Pen and paper.
Timing Once.

Split a sheet of paper into two. In the left-hand column, write down a series of key-words or short sentences that describe how you appear to the other stakeholders when you are negotiating. Think about how you speak to them, how you act, what you talk about, and so on.

In the right-hand column, perform the same exercise, but describe how you behave when you have gone out for a meal with some old friends. Look at the differences between the two. Are there ways you could move the experience for the stakeholders towards that of your friends?

Feedback I am not suggesting that the stakeholders become your friends, nor am I suggesting that you go out for a meal with them – although that wouldn't be a bad idea. What would be very valuable in negotiation is if the stakeholders caught a glimpse of the real you, the one you show to your friends, not the artificial front most of us put on for formal events like a negotiation.

Anything you can do that helps the other stakeholders to get to know (and hopefully like) you as a person will help with the trust that makes it so much easier to achieve win–win. The more you can become a real person to them, the less likely they are to stab you in the back and the more likely they are to extend human courtesy and warmth. This is why face-to-face contact is so important in negotiation – and although people have fallen in love via e-mail or online chat, you are much more likely to get on in a reasonable timescale if you are in the physical presence of the other person.

Outcome Make it hard for the other stakeholders to be impersonally nasty to you. If they know and like you as a person, they are much more likely to help you to a win–win outcome.

Variations None.

Strategic   ✪✪✪✪
Intuitive   ✪✪✪✪
Process   ✪
Fun   ✪✪✪

5.75 | *Price movement*

Preparation None.
Running time Five minutes.
Resources Pen and paper.
Timing Once.

Movement isn't always a feature of negotiation (at least on your part), but it may have to be. This exercise gives some preparation on dealing with movements in price.

1. What is wrong with this opening remark: 'Our normal rate is £1500'?

2. If you had to accept a movement of £500 in price, would you take it all at once or in stages – and if so, how would it be broken up?

3. How can you structure pricing to protect the amount you want?

Spend a couple of minutes jotting down answers before going any further.

Feedback You don't have to move on price of course – in fact, it may be one of the last variables you let shift – but in some cases it will be necessary. When it is, make sure that you get something back – say 'Well, I could squeeze another percentage point, if you can...'. (See *There's always an 'if'*, 5.64.) In the first example, the word 'normal' is dangerous. Although it's not as much of a give-away as saying 'But of course it's negotiable', it is still giving something away right at the start. Your pricing is sensible and justified, so don't qualify it, be proud of it.

Structuring movement in a big lump gives the other stakeholder the impression you've got plenty of room for manoeuvre. Go for decreasingly small increments (say £300, then £100, then £50), to emphasize that you've little left to give – and to give three movements for the price of one. As the third question suggests, you can also structure the pricing to protect your margins. If you have an amount you absolutely must get, by adding a number of secondary elements to the product or service that can be squeezed relatively painlessly, you can ensure that you have plenty of margin left.

Outcome Handling price movement will be demanded in many negotiations.

Variations It helps if you get the starting price right – see *Starting prices*, 5.23.

Strategic	✪
Intuitive	✪
Process	✪
Fun	✪✪

6

OTHER SOURCES

FINDING OUT MORE

Negotiation brings in a wide range of skills centred on communication and human endeavour. *Instant Negotiation* is a great toolkit for the negotiator, but being more widely read, particularly in associated areas like creativity, stress management and research, will be of great help. The books listed here are designed to expand your negotiating resources.

An easy way to get hold of many of the recommended books is through the Creativity Unleashed online bookshop, which specializes in business and creativity books – see **http://www.cul.co.uk/books**.

GENERAL

Gavin Kennedy, *Everything is Negotiable*, Arrow, 1997
An excellent beginner's guide to negotiating. The starting premise is a counter to everyone's nervous assumption that it has to be stated in advance that some (and only some) aspects of a deal are negotiable. Kennedy's philosophy is that you invert this and work on the assumption that everything is negotiable. A very practical and readable introduction.

Robert Maddux, *Successful Negotiation*, Kogan Page, 1988
A simple, quick guide for absolute beginners to the negotiating process. This book, in the Better Management Skills series, uses checklists and mini-questionnaires to help the reader to assess their position. Subtitled 'How to create a win–win situation', it uses fictional examples to work through each of its main propositions.

John Mattock and Jöns Ehrenborg, *How to be a Better Negotiator*, Kogan Page, 1996
A series of sections on the main contributors to successful negotiation lead you through this easy-to-read book. There is plenty of focus on the cultural and emotional aspects of negotiation and the management of the game plan. A good general guide.

David Oliver, *101 Ways to Negotiate More Effectively*, Kogan Page, 1996
While the '101 ways' is a rather over-stretched concept, it doesn't get in the way of this being a very effective book of lessons for negotiators. Chances are, whatever your experience, you'll find something in here that is useful.

Howard Raiffa, *The Art and Science of Negotiation*, Harvard University Press, 1985
A classic book on negotiation that tries to endow a more scientific approach of 'negotiation analysis' to the process. A combination of psychology, decision theory and game theory is used to dig into just what is happening in negotiation. Not the world's most practical book, but valuable background reading for any negotiator.

CREATIVITY

Good negotiation has a strong streak of creativity. Knowing just which variables to tweak or, even better, pulling new variables into the equation is an essential skill for the negotiator, and this is a creative art. Luckily, creativity is something than can be enhanced with appropriate techniques, which these books cover.

Tony and Barry Buzan, *The Mind Map Book*, BBC Books, 1993
A beautifully illustrated guide to the use of mind maps to take notes, structure ideas and aid memory. Valuable in negotiation, mind maps make sure you never lose track of the current position. Written by Tony Buzan, the developer of the mind map concept, and his brother.

Brian Clegg, *Instant Brainpower*, Kogan Page, 1999
This book in the Instants series is an ideal complement to *Instant Negotiation*, as it builds on some key skills that are essential to negotiation – memory, knowledge handling and innate creative ability. A wide range of exercises make enhancing your thinking skills enjoyable and effective.

Brian Clegg and Paul Birch, *Instant Creativity*, Kogan Page, 1999
This book in the Instants series provides over 70 different techniques for coming up with new ideas and solving problems, each designed to be used with the minimum of fuss in an instant.

Brian Clegg and Paul Birch, *Imagination Engineering*, FT Knowledge, 2000
A toolkit for business creativity, providing a practical but enjoyable guide to making creativity work. Introduces a four-stage process for business creativity, equally applicable for a five-minute session or a week concentrating on a single problem. Plenty of depth but fun, too.

Edward de Bono, *Serious Creativity*, HarperCollins, 1996
A wide-ranging book from the best-known UK creativity guru. de Bono invented the term 'lateral thinking' and here he explores the benefits of creativity and describes his personally preferred techniques. A dry book, but one that pulls together all de Bono's key work on the subject.

Roger von Oech, *A Whack on the Side of the Head*, Warner Books, 1983
In total contrast to de Bono, von Oech's laid-back Californian style attacks the blockers to creativity in an enjoyable way. It sometimes feels more like a humour book than a management text, but is none the worse for this, and there's a serious message under the gloss.

RESEARCH

Brian Clegg, *Mining the Internet*, Kogan Page, 1999
The Internet is a superb source for obtaining the information that is a crucial background to any negotiation, but finding the right information can be near impossible. Rather than provide a dated guide to the Web, this popular book provides the skills needed to find your way around the Internet, using the Web, e-mails, newsgroups and more to get to the information you need.

Reva Vasch, *Researching Online for Dummies*, IDG, 1998
One of the yellow 'dummies' guides, particularly focused on information-gathering online. More for the information specialists than *Mining the Internet*, but a very effective guide for professional researchers supporting negotiations and for those who want to go into the depths of research technology.

SELLING

Although it should be emphasized that the negotiator is not a pure salesperson, there is a strong overlap between some aspects of negotiating and some aspects of selling. The gurus of sales have a lot to say that is of extreme value to any form of negotiation. These are very valuable books for any negotiator.

Jay Abraham, *Getting Everything You Can out of All You've Got*, Piatkus Books, 2000
A paean of the wonders of selling from the man aptly referred to as the greatest marketing expert alive. Abraham's style is sometimes irritatingly inspirational, but his content is second to none. This book is almost guaranteed to ensure success in the way you go about selling yourself, your business and your negotiating points.

Brian Clegg, *Capturing Customers' Hearts*, FT Prentice Hall, 2000
This book examines what it is about a company, its products, its brands and its people that wins over customers. It examines 12 components of charisma – the property that enables a company or product to sell itself to the customer. Capturing the other stakeholders' hearts at the negotiating table is quite a challenge, but it can pay off handsomely.

Richard Denny, *Selling to Win*, Kogan Page, 1997
A very practical, very readable book that takes away the mystery from selling. Full of useful insights, there's a tried and tested technique here for every occasion.

MOTIVATION

Motivation is a powerful underlying skill for the negotiator. In a selling negotiation, your aim is to bring the other stakeholders round to your way of thinking. In exploration, you will want everyone to reach the best solution. In either case, a great negotiator is not just concerned with fighting his or her own corner, but with giving the other stakeholders the motivation to proceed.

John Allan, *How to be Better at Motivating People*, Kogan Page, 1996
An Industrial Society-backed guide to motivation. Good use of case studies and tips makes this an excellent choice if you want to expand on the background in the opening chapters of *Instant Motivation* (see below).

Brian Clegg, *Instant Motivation*, Kogan Page, 2000
A companion volume to *Instant Negotiation*, *Instant Motivation* provides over 70 techniques and skills to get individuals, teams and large groups better in line with your aspirations. An excellent adjunct to this book.

Richard Denny, *Motivate to Win*, Kogan Page, 1993
Don't be put off by the relative age of this book, the content hasn't dated. Denny has a very charismatic approach to motivation, and puts the message across well. It's a personal approach, so some may not like it – but it's worth a look. If you are only going for one Denny, though, go for *Selling to Win* (see page 131).

David Firth, *How to Make Work Fun*, Gower, 1995
David Firth's book explores the whole area of fun and work and its implications for motivation. The A to Z format seems a little forced occasionally, but makes it easy to dip into. While not always directly practical, it's a great source of inspiration.

Patrick Forsyth, *30 Minutes to Motivate Your Staff*, Kogan Page, 1998
Part of a pocket book series putting across the basics of the subject – handy if you'd like a bit more than our introductory chapters can give, but haven't time for a Denny or an Allan.

Robert Heller, *Motivating People*, Dorling Kindersley, 1998
A handy pocket guide to motivation in the heavily illustrated DK style. Some of the approaches are a trifle old-fashioned, but overall a good introduction to the subject.

Michael Leapman, *The Last Days of the Beeb*, Coronet 1987
Leapman's inside view of the BBC before the major reorganizations that turned it into a modern business is a classic case study in how not to motivate. Well worth reading.

Ricardo Semler, *Maverick!*, Arrow, 1994
One of the best books ever written about motivation. It's not a textbook, but the biography of a company. Despite being located in Brazil during runaway inflation and with potentially difficult unions, Semler took a disgruntled workforce and totally changed their motivation by making their workplace a place where they wanted to be.

STRESS MANAGEMENT

Brian Clegg, *Instant Stress Management*, Kogan Page, 2000
One of the most popular titles in the Instant series, *Instant Stress Management* helps to get the stress of negotiation under control. Recognizing that one of the main stressors is time pressure, it provides over 70 techniques that can be taken on board in a few minutes, handling stress when and where it occurs.

Cary L Cooper, Rachel Cooper and Lynn Eaker, *Living with Stress*, Penguin, 1991
A good exploration of stress, what it is and where it comes from. Although not specifically business-oriented, this book spends quite a lot of time on workplace stress, including some slightly dated but nonetheless useful research. Includes DIY stress questionnaires to assess your condition.

Lynn Fossum, *Managing Anxiety*, Kogan Page, 1993
A quick guide to the nature of anxiety and how to conquer it. Fossum's book is short and has plenty of practical exercises to reduce this key component of stress.

Brenda O'Hanlon, *Stress, The Commonsense Approach*, Newleaf, 1998
A good pocketbook giving a general overview of stress and ways of dealing with it. Gives rather a lot of space to alternative treatments and therapy, but otherwise well balanced.

David Ashton, *The 12-Week Executive Health Plan*, Kogan Page, 1993
Good health is one of the cornerstones of being able to manage stress (and survive negotiations). This readable book, which manages to avoid the tendency of the health movement to work with the fad-of-the-moment, is a good guide to getting something practical done about improving your health.

TIME MANAGEMENT

Time management is the Cinderella of management skills. It seems dowdy and unattractive, but getting it right is at the heart of so much business success, including negotiation. These books look at putting time management in its right place, making it less of a chore and more of an essential feature of life.

Brian Clegg, *The Chameleon Manager*, Butterworth Heinemann, 1998
This book takes the concept of time management into the wider sphere of gaining the skills needed to thrive in the workplace of the new millennium. It identifies management of creativity, communication and knowledge – all valuable to negotiation – as the key requirements to working your way.

Brian Clegg, *Instant Time Management*, Kogan Page, 1999
A companion volume in the Instant series, *Instant Time Management* provides a host of techniques for improving your time management without taking up too much time over it. Good time management enables you to deliver on your promises and ensures that your negotiation doesn't suffer from timing delays and disasters.

Marion E. Haynes, *Make Every Minute Count*, Kogan Page, 2000
In the Creating Success series, this in the only one of these books that is US-written – but the subject varies little between countries. Even more check lists and questionnaires than Smith's book; this is an excellent way of getting started on the subject.

Ted Johns, *Perfect Time Management*, Arrow, 1994
A handy pocketbook giving an overview of time management practice from a very pragmatic viewpoint. Varies between background and quite a lot of detail (eg suggested forms for the agenda of a meeting).

Lothar J Seiwert, *Managing Your Time*, Kogan Page, 1989
A very visual book with lots of diagrams and plans and cartoons – it'll either impress you (as it has apparently more than 300,000 readers) or leave you cold. Particularly helpful if you like very specific guidance and information as juicy snippets.

Jane Smith, *How to be a Better Time Manager*, Kogan Page, 1997
An Industrial Society-sponsored volume, Smith's book takes an easy-to-read, no-nonsense approach to time management. A fair number of checklists and short questionnaires to fill in along the way, if you like that style.

APPENDIX:
THE SELECTOR

SELECTION TABLES

This appendix contains a series of tables to help you to select an exercise to do right now. The first table, the random selector is for when you'd like something unexpected. The other tables help to highlight a particular characteristic of an exercise, like applicability to process, or fun.

THE RANDOM SELECTOR

Take a watch with a second hand and note the number the second hand is pointing at now. Take that number technique from the list of 60 below. A few of the exercises assume you have completed another already – if you hit one of these and haven't done the preliminaries, either do the other exercise first or pick again.

No.	Ref.	Title	No.	Ref.	Title
1	5.1	Lifetime value	27	5.36	I'll be honest…
2	5.2	Taking notes	28	5.37	When you lose your temper
3	5.3	Web research			
4	5.4	The agreement space	29	5.38	Creative negotiation
5	5.6	Are they telling the truth?	30	5.39	Beautiful barter
6	5.7	Upping the game	31	5.40	Delightful deals
7	5.9	Talking yourself down	32	5.41	Personality types
8	5.11	Go casual	33	5.42	Wooing them
9	5.12	Using emotion	34	5.43	Selling your wider strengths
10	5.13	Competitive pressure			
11	5.15	The power of print	35	5.44	Common ground
12	5.16	It's yours right now	36	5.47	Little successes
13	5.18	Exploring trust	37	5.48	Slowing the pace
14	5.20	Sophisticated option evaluation	38	5.49	Throwing in the condiment
			39	5.50	Deadlines – the movable feast
15	5.21	Options with guts			
16	5.22	Reading upside down (no, really!)	40	5.51	Remote negotiation
			41	5.52	Make them feel good about the deal
17	5.23	Starting prices			
18	5.24	Playing poker	42	5.53	Plotting the journey
19	5.25	Another lever	43	5.54	Using silence
20	5.26	Your USP	44	5.55	Cornered rats
21	5.27	Setting targets	45	5.58	Body language
22	5.30	Knowing the opposition	46	5.59	Don't leave the next step in their hands
23	5.32	Cut the aggro			
24	5.33	Which way?	47	5.60	Say what?
25	5.34	Terms of endearment	48	5.62	Principles
26	5.35	Future visions	49	5.63	Aim high to get more

50	5.64	There's always an 'if'	55	5.70	I haven't the authority…
51	5.65	Knowing your products and services	56	5.71	Appearing naïve
			57	5.72	Liking the opposition
52	5.66	Doing a special	58	5.73	Stakeholder customer
53	5.67	Slicing the salami	59	5.74	Being you
54	5.68	Walkies!	60	5.75	Price movement

TECHNIQUES IN TIMING ORDER

This table sorts the techniques by the suggested timings. Those at the top take the longest, those towards the bottom are the quickest.

Ref.	Title	Ref.	Title
Evening		5.26	Your USP
5.61	You won't win them all	5.30	Knowing the opposition
		5.39	Beautiful barter
Variable		5.43	Selling your wider strengths
5.11	Go casual	5.44	Common ground
5.45	Rehearsing for success	5.49	Throwing in the condiment
		5.58	Body language
30 minutes		5.59	Don't leave the next step in their hands
5.3	Web research	5.60	Say what?
5.17	Getting endorsements	5.63	Aim high to get more
5.27	Setting targets		
		5 minutes	
20 minutes		5.1	Lifetime value
5.2	Taking notes	5.6	Are they telling the truth?
5.20	Sophisticated option evaluation	5.8	Paper mountains
		5.10	Waiting room
15 minutes		5.12	Using emotion
5.4	The agreement space	5.13	Competitive pressure
5.18	Exploring trust	5.22	Reading upside down
5.19	Basic option evaluation	5.24	Playing poker
5.21	Options with guts	5.28	Play that back
5.38	Creative negotiation	5.29	Subverting a meeting
5.53	Plotting the journey	5.31	Broken CD
5.54	Using silence	5.32	Cut the aggro
5.57	Coffee and doughnuts	5.33	Which way?
5.65	Knowing your products and services	5.34	Terms of endearment
5.68	Walkies!	5.35	Future visions
		5.36	I'll be honest
10 minutes		5.37	When you lose your temper
5.5	Hearing what they really say	5.41	Personality types
5.7	Upping the game	5.48	Slowing the pace
5.15	The power of print		
5.23	Starting prices		
5.25	Another lever		

5.50	Deadlines – the movable feast
5.51	Remote negotiation
5.55	Cornered rats
5.62	Principles
5.64	There's always an 'if'
5.66	Doing a special
5.67	Slicing the salami
5.69	Good guy/bad guy
5.72	Liking the opposition
5.73	Stakeholder customer
5.74	Being you
5.75	Price movement

2 minutes

5.9	Talking yourself down
5.14	Breathing is good for you
5.16	It's yours right now
5.40	Delightful deals
5.42	Wooing them
5.46	Yes… eventually
5.47	Little successes
5.52	Make them feel good about the deal
5.56	Ask, ask and ask again
5.70	I haven't the authority…
5.71	Appearing naïve

TECHNIQUES IN FREQUENCY ORDER

This table sorts the techniques by the frequency order. Those at the top are undertaken most frequently, those towards the bottom once only.

Ref.	Title		Ref.	Title
Daily			5.9	Talking yourself down
5.8	Paper mountains		5.11	Go casual
			5.12	Using emotion
Regularly			5.13	Competitive pressure
5.10	Waiting room		5.15	The power of print
5.14	Breathing is good for you		5.16	It's yours right now
5.45	Rehearsing for success		5.17	Getting endorsements
5.56	Ask, ask and ask again		5.18	Exploring trust
5.57	Coffee and doughnuts		5.19	Basic option evaluation
5.68	Walkies!		5.20	Sophisticated option evaluation
			5.21	Options with guts
Special			5.23	Starting prices
5.61	You won't win them all		5.24	Playing poker
5.69	Good guy/bad guy		5.25	Another lever
			5.26	Your USP
Several times			5.27	Setting targets
5.2	Taking notes		5.29	Subverting a meeting
5.5	Hearing what they really say		5.30	Knowing the opposition
5.22	Reading upside down		5.31	Broken CD
5.28	Play that back		5.32	Cut the aggro
5.46	Yes… eventually		5.33	Which way?
5.47	Little successes		5.34	Terms of endearment
			5.35	Future visions
Once			5.36	I'll be honest…
5.1	Lifetime value		5.37	When you lose your temper
5.3	Web research		5.38	Creative negotiation
5.4	The agreement space			
5.6	Are they telling the truth?			
5.7	Upping the game			

5.39	Beautiful barter
5.40	Delightful deals
5.41	Personality types
5.42	Wooing them
5.43	Selling your wider strengths
5.44	Common ground
5.48	Slowing the pace
5.49	Throwing in the condiment
5.50	Deadlines – the movable feast
5.51	Remote negotiation
5.52	Make them feel good about the deal
5.53	Plotting the journey
5.54	Using silence
5.55	Cornered rats
5.58	Body language

5.59	Don't leave the next step in their hands
5.60	Say what?
5.62	Principles
5.63	Aim high to get more
5.64	There's always an 'if'
5.65	Knowing your products and services
5.66	Doing a special
5.67	Slicing the salami
5.70	I haven't the authority…
5.71	Appearing naïve
5.72	Liking the opposition
5.73	Stakeholder customer
5.74	Being you
5.75	Price movement

TECHNIQUES BY STRATEGIC RATING

This table sorts the techniques by the individual star ratings attached to each. Those at the top are most strategic, those at the bottom are most tactical.

Ref.	Title
✪✪✪✪	
5.1	Lifetime value
5.3	Web research
5.14	Breathing is good for you
5.18	Exploring trust
5.25	Another lever
5.26	Your USP
5.27	Setting targets
5.30	Knowing the opposition
5.33	Which way?
5.41	Personality types
5.45	Rehearsing for success
5.52	Make them feel good about the deal
5.53	Plotting the journey
5.56	Ask, ask and ask again
5.61	You won't win them all
5.62	Principles
5.73	Stakeholder customer
5.74	Being you

Ref.	Title
✪✪✪	
5.4	The agreement space
5.8	Paper mountains
5.12	Using emotion
5.15	The power of print
5.23	Starting prices
5.34	Terms of endearment
5.39	Beautiful barter
5.42	Wooing them
5.44	Common ground
5.58	Body language
5.72	Liking the opposition
✪✪	
5.22	Reading upside down
5.28	Play that back
5.29	Subverting a meeting
5.36	I'll be honest…
5.37	When you lose your temper
5.38	Creative negotiation
5.40	Delightful deals
5.51	Remote negotiation

5.59	Don't leave the next step in their hands	5.35	Future visions
5.63	Aim high to get more	5.43	Selling your wider strengths
5.68	Walkies!	5.46	Yes… eventually
✪		5.47	Little successes
5.2	Taking notes	5.48	Slowing the pace
5.5	Hearing what they really say	5.49	Throwing in the condiment
5.6	Are they telling the truth?	5.50	Deadlines – the movable feast
5.7	Upping the game	5.54	Using silence
5.9	Talking yourself down	5.55	Cornered rats
5.10	Waiting room	5.57	Coffee and doughnuts
5.11	Go casual	5.60	Say what?
5.13	Competitive pressure	5.64	There's always an 'if'
5.16	It's yours right now	5.65	Knowing your products and services
5.17	Getting endorsements	5.66	Doing a special
5.19	Basic option evaluation	5.67	Slicing the salami
5.20	Sophisticated option evaluation	5.69	Good guy/bad guy
5.21	Options with guts	5.70	I haven't the authority…
5.24	Playing poker	5.71	Appearing naïve
5.31	Broken CD	5.75	Price movement
5.32	Cut the aggro		

TECHNIQUES BY INTUITIVE RATING

This table sorts the techniques by the individual star ratings attached to each. Those at the top are most intuitive; those at the bottom are most logical.

Ref. ✪✪✪✪	Title	Ref. ✪✪✪	Title
5.6	Are they telling the truth?	5.5	Hearing what they really say
5.9	Talking yourself down	5.7	Upping the game
5.12	Using emotion	5.11	Go casual
5.16	It's yours right now	5.13	Competitive pressure
5.24	Playing poker	5.14	Breathing is good for you
5.32	Cut the aggro	5.15	The power of print
5.39	Beautiful barter	5.17	Getting endorsements
5.40	Delightful deals	5.21	Options with guts
5.42	Wooing them	5.23	Starting prices
5.47	Little successes	5.26	Your USP
5.52	Make them feel good about the deal	5.28	Play that back
5.57	Coffee and doughnuts	5.31	Broken CD
5.58	Body language	5.34	Terms of endearment
5.62	Principles	5.35	Future visions
5.74	Being you	5.36	I'll be honest…
		5.38	Creative negotiation

5.41	Personality types		✪	
5.44	Common ground		5.1	Lifetime value
5.48	Slowing the pace		5.3	Web research
5.50	Deadlines – the movable feast		5.4	The agreement space
5.54	Using silence		5.8	Paper mountains
5.55	Cornered rats		5.10	Waiting room
5.61	You won't win them all		5.19	Basic option evaluation
5.63	Aim high to get more		5.20	Sophisticated option evaluation
5.66	Doing a special		5.22	Reading upside down
5.68	Walkies!		5.29	Subverting a meeting
5.69	Good guy/bad guy		5.30	Knowing the opposition
5.72	Liking the opposition		5.37	When you lose your temper
5.73	Stakeholder customer		5.45	Rehearsing for success
✪✪			5.49	Throwing in the condiment
5.2	Taking notes		5.56	Ask, ask and ask again
5.18	Exploring trust		5.59	Don't leave the next step in their hands
5.25	Another lever		5.60	Say what?
5.27	Setting targets		5.64	There's always an 'if'
5.33	Which way?		5.65	Knowing your products and services
5.43	Selling your wider strengths		5.67	Slicing the salami
5.46	Yes… eventually		5.75	Price movement
5.51	Remote negotiation			
5.53	Plotting the journey			
5.70	I haven't the authority…			
5.71	Appearing naïve			

TECHNIQUES BY PROCESS RATING

This table sorts the techniques by the individual star ratings attached to each. Those at the top are most process oriented; those at the bottom are most communication oriented.

Ref.	Title		Ref.	Title
✪✪✪✪			5.25	Another lever
5.1	Lifetime value		5.26	Your USP
5.2	Taking notes		5.27	Setting targets
5.3	Web research		5.30	Knowing the opposition
5.4	The agreement space		5.34	Terms of endearment
5.8	Paper mountains		5.38	Creative negotiation
5.11	Go casual		5.39	Beautiful barter
5.14	Breathing is good for you		5.45	Rehearsing for success
5.19	Basic option evaluation		5.47	Little successes
5.20	Sophisticated option evaluation		5.53	Plotting the journey
5.21	Options with guts		5.56	Ask, ask and ask again
5.23	Starting prices		5.61	You won't win them all

5.68	Walkies!
✪✪✪	
5.7	Upping the game
5.10	Waiting room
5.17	Getting endorsements
5.18	Exploring trust
5.22	Reading upside down
5.33	Which way?
5.37	When you lose your temper
5.40	Delightful deals
5.41	Personality types
5.48	Slowing the pace
5.49	Throwing in the condiment
5.50	Deadlines – the movable feast
5.55	Cornered rats
5.57	Coffee and doughnuts
5.59	Don't leave the next step in their hands
5.62	Principles
5.63	Aim high to get more
5.65	Knowing your products and services
5.67	Slicing the salami
5.69	Good guy/bad guy
5.72	Liking the opposition
5.73	Stakeholder customer
✪✪	
5.13	Competitive pressure
5.15	The power of print
5.29	Subverting a meeting

5.42	Wooing them
5.46	Yes… eventually
5.66	Doing a special
✪	
5.5	Hearing what they really say
5.6	Are they telling the truth?
5.9	Talking yourself down
5.12	Using emotion
5.16	It's yours right now
5.24	Playing poker
5.28	Play that back
5.31	Broken CD
5.32	Cut the aggro
5.35	Future visions
5.36	I'll be honest…
5.43	Selling your wider strengths
5.44	Common ground
5.51	Remote negotiation
5.52	Make them feel good about the deal
5.54	Using silence
5.58	Body language
5.60	Say what?
5.64	There's always an 'if'
5.66	Doing a special
5.70	I haven't the authority…
5.71	Appearing naïve
5.74	Being you
5.75	Price movement

TECHNIQUES BY FUN RATING

This table sorts the techniques by the individual star ratings attached to each. Those at the top have the highest star rating, those at the bottom the lowest.

Ref.	Title
✪✪✪✪	
5.22	Reading upside down
5.38	Creative negotiation
5.40	Delightful deals
5.57	Coffee and doughnuts
5.61	You won't win them all
5.68	Walkies!

Ref.	Title
✪✪✪	
5.2	Taking notes
5.3	Web research
5.8	Paper mountains
5.11	Go casual
5.12	Using emotion
5.13	Competitive pressure

5.14   Breathing is good for you
5.16   It's yours right now
5.18   Exploring trust
5.23   Starting prices
5.24   Playing poker
5.35   Future visions
5.39   Beautiful barter
5.42   Wooing them
5.45   Rehearsing for success
5.47   Little successes
5.53   Plotting the journey
5.69   Good guy/bad guy
5.71   Appearing naïve
5.72   Liking the opposition
5.73   Stakeholder customer
5.74   Being you

❷❷

5.1   Lifetime value
5.4   The agreement space
5.5   Hearing what they really say
5.6   Are they telling the truth?
5.7   Upping the game
5.9   Talking yourself down
5.10   Waiting room
5.15   The power of print
5.19   Basic option evaluation
5.20   Sophisticated option evaluation
5.21   Options with guts
5.25   Another lever
5.26   Your USP
5.27   Setting targets
5.28   Play that back
5.29   Subverting a meeting
5.30   Knowing the opposition

5.31   Broken CD
5.32   Cut the aggro
5.33   Which way?
5.34   Terms of endearment
5.36   I'll be honest…
5.41   Personality types
5.43   Selling your wider strengths
5.44   Common ground
5.46   Yes… eventually
5.48   Slowing the pace
5.49   Throwing in the condiment
5.50   Deadlines – the movable feast
5.51   Remote negotiation
5.55   Cornered rats
5.58   Body language
5.59   Don't leave the next step in their hands
5.60   Say what?
5.62   Principles
5.63   Aim high to get more
5.64   There's always an 'if'
5.65   Knowing your products and services
5.66   Doing a special
5.67   Slicing the salami
5.70   I haven't the authority…
5.75   Price movement

❶

5.17   Getting endorsements
5.37   When you lose your temper
5.52   Make them feel good about the deal
5.54   Using silence
5.56   Ask, ask and ask again